D0175138

A Father...
A Son...
and a
Three-Mile Run

A Father...
A Son...
and a
Three-Mile
Run
Keith J. Leenhouts

ZONDERVAN
PUBLISHING HOUSE   OF THE ZONDERVAN CORPORATION
GRAND RAPIDS, MICHIGAN 49506

A FATHER . . . A SON . . . AND A THREE-MILE RUN

This love story is dedicated to
Bill, our son,
In his nineteenth year and to his
Mother, Audrey,
In the twentieth year of our marriage and to
Dave and Jim,
Our other sons, in their fifteenth and thirteenth years

The day the race was run

Contents

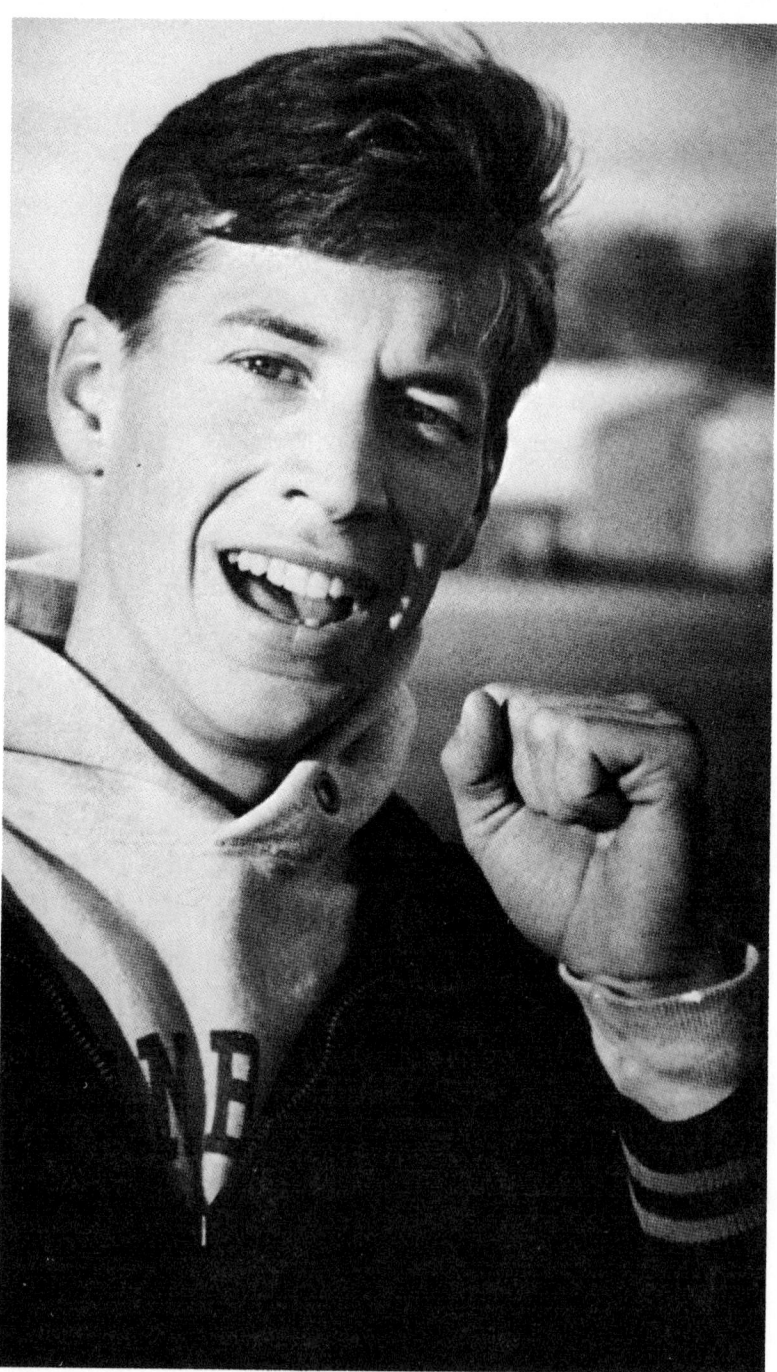

Preface

WE OFTEN THINK OF THE LATE SIXTIES AND EARLY seventies as years when an outbreak of "generation gaps" occurred, when children and parents became increasingly alienated from each other, when family and societal relationships as we had known them generally broke down. Many, then, would say that the awesome father-son relationship described in this book just could not have happened during this turbulent era.

It did. And I am convinced that hundreds of thousands of fathers and sons in this country have experienced or are experiencing a similar relationship to that which our son, Bill, and I lived for eighteen great years.

For the hundreds of thousands of fathers and sons who have not been fortunate enough to enjoy such a beautiful experience, it is our hope that this book will help just a few to begin a new life and love between them.

But this book is not intended to be a manual or a "how-to" set of instructions for a "successful" father-son relationship. Rather, it is a simple, true story of love.

KEITH J. LEENHOUTS

Eagles Nest Lake
Soudan, Minnesota

Acknowledgments

Obviously, THERE MUST BE A COMPELLING REASON for someone who is not a professional writer to write a book. Especially when it is written during a vacation. There was indeed such a motivation. I wanted Bill and me to have a story about our life together; I wrote it just for the two of us.

After Bill read it, we decided to submit it to our friends at the *Reader's Digest*. We considered doing this under assumed names, then decided against it. The Digest published the article, "Race for Love," in October 1974. They advised us to submit the book to Zondervan Publishing House and we did.

Zondervan liked the book and agreed to publish it. Thus the original reason for writing the story has been extended.

Since the time I could devote to the book was very limited, I would like to express my deep gratitude and appreciation to Paul Friede and Jim Ruark for their time and extraordinary talent in the final editing, composition, and arrangement of the manuscript. They were — and are — great!

It is my hope that many fathers will write a story about life with their sons. Most, maybe all of them, will be what I first intended — a book just between a father and a son. I fully anticipate that the next two books I write, about sons Dave and Jim, will be just that.

However, some of the fathers who write such books might also share them with others. If they do, let's hope that they make our nation far more aware of one of the greatest gifts of all: fatherhood.

I
From the Ashes of Defeat

ONE HUNDRED AND FORTY HIGH-SCHOOL RUNNERS fidgeted nervously at the long starting line, anxiety and desire momentarily aging their young faces as they contemplated the lonely, grueling three-mile cross-country run that lay ahead.

All were dedicated athletes who had run between five and fifteen miles every day for most of their high-school years to prepare themselves for this climactic moment, the running of the 1972 Michigan High-School Cross-Country Championship. Each had beaten literally thousands of other young men in a series of Regional races to get this final chance to win "All-State" honors. Yes, for the 140 young men now crouched tensely in the starting position, this was indeed a special race — the culmination of years of dedication, preparation, and sustained desire.

But for one — a spindly, awkward-looking boy named Bill — and for me, his father, the significance of this race reached far beyond the mere pursuit of an athletic victory. For us this was a race of love — a love and a relationship that perhaps belong to a distant and lost generation, not to a generation of so many rejected children, rejected parents, and rejected values.

The fact that Bill had even qualified for this race was itself a majestic manifestation of the awesome power of this tough, realistic, and tender father-son love. This was a love and a relationship born out of duty and obligation, nurtured by the positive influence of others, and made strong by eighteen years of continuous battles against agonizing, often near-crushing academic, athletic, and emotional defeats.

I looked at Bill crouched at the starting line, his face twisted by anxiety and desire, and knew that for the next three miles he would battle not only 139 of Michigan's best high-school runners, but also a lifetime of overwhelming odds, defeats, and failures.

Cross-country is among the most grueling of sports. It is strangely uplifting to talk to football and basketball players and tell them your son is in cross-country. Inevitably the heroes of the glamor sports say, "Man, that really takes guts. I could never do that." Stated simply, cross-country means running several miles across land that is largely unimproved and unchanged from the way nature made and preserved it.

The excited noise of the crowd turned to tense silence as the starter raised his gun. I wondered if this, Bill's last high-school race, would end in a long-awaited victory of the heart or in another, perhaps final, crushing defeat of his spirit and soul.

Crack! A rainbow of 20 seven-man teams, clad in colored T-shirts and shorts, burst from the line. Crack! Crack! Two more shots split the cold, crisp November air, signaling a false start. Two runners had started before the gun.

"All right, men, relax a little. You've got a long way to go!" said the starter, a soft-spoken, grandfatherly gentleman. The "thinclads," many already glistening with sweat, jogged back to the starting line, twisting their necks, flapping their arms, and loosening up their legs to prevent a sudden, incapacitating tightening of their muscles, a "charley horse."

Bill looked pale and nervous as the runners regrouped at the line. *Does he really belong here?* I wondered. *Certainly most of the other runners are more skillful. Others are endowed with greater strength and speed. Cases can be made for nearly all the others in terms of feet, inches, and miles-per-hour, but has anyone ever invented a scale to measure the strength of a young man's heart? What term can be used to pinpoint the limits of desire?*

It's a funny thing about desire — no one can measure it accurately, yet it rarely changes. It was there in the skinny six-year-old who failed in school. It is there now in the eighteen-year-old near-man. And when his sandy brown hair is flecked with gray and the waves look like little snowdrifts, the desire won't have waned or grown stale with the years.

But could his desire alone carry him to his dream, his goal of being an All-State runner? He would have to finish in the top fifteen out of these 140 runners to earn that honor.

IMPOSSIBLE. BILL HAD FINISHED A DISTANT EIGHTH in his Regional race and, by comparing his time with the runners who had qualified in the other nineteen Regionals, he theoretically should finish in the lowest one-fourth. Another defeat seemed inevitable.

In his eighteen short years Bill had already suffered so many. Grade school, for example, had been a nightmare for him, six years of failure and ridicule.

Though he tried very hard, six-year-old Bill just could not grasp the extremely important first-grade reading fundamentals. So after talking it over with Bill and his teacher, we all decided he should repeat first grade. Bill didn't complain about this decision and tried even harder to achieve, but still he was unable to learn at the same pace as his younger classmates, who added to his burden by ridiculing him for "flunking."

When he was only nine, unbeknownst to him his third-grade teacher labeled, branded, and placed him on the academic dump heap. She had called my wife and me into her office for the first of what proved to be many special conferences. We approached it with fear and concern. Had Bill misbehaved? Wasn't he trying? Didn't he care about school?

After a few moments of polite small talk, his teacher, a plump, bespectacled, stern-looking woman, came directly to the point.

"I'm afraid I have some very unpleasant news for you, Judge and Mrs. Leenhouts," she said, her severe but genuinely concerned voice trembling a little. "Your son will never be able to attend college. He just does not have the mental ability. He certainly tries hard, and no child is more lovable, but he just can't achieve academically. I'm very sorry to have to tell you this. I know it must be a terrible shock."

I leaned back heavily in the stiff-backed wooden chair, breathed deeply, and said softly, "Oh, is that all? We were so afraid you had some really bad news for us."

Her concerned expression quickly turned to bewilderment, then disbelief as she asked, "Isn't it important to you that your son goes to college? Don't you feel he *must*? After all, you're the judge of our city. What will people think if the judge's son doesn't go to college? Wouldn't you be embarrassed?"

She was so sincere, so upset and concerned, that I repressed a laugh of relief as I explained that my ego did not need feeding by a son who went to college. Nor was I concerned that his academic achievements somehow would affect my "reputation." We certainly hoped Bill could go to college someday, but much more importantly we wanted him to grow up with a love for the Lord and his fellowman and we wanted him always to do his best.

Bill continued to struggle almost desperately. A paralyzed muscle in his left eye — a temporary, childhood condition that caused him to suffer double vision and severe perceptual problems — made the learning process even more difficult. Two more years of conferences about academic "failures" followed.

Finally, in the sixth grade Bill's teacher, a young, understanding woman, called us in and said, "Judge and Mrs. Leenhouts, I'm sorry to have to tell you this, but Bill isn't trying anymore — he has given up completely and I'm not really surprised. In fact, I'm more surprised that he didn't give up long ago. I've talked with his other teachers and we have all observed the same thing. All of us have wondered how long this determined little boy could maintain such tremendous desire and keep trying so hard when he accomplished so little. He has worked so hard for so many years and has nothing to show for it. Now he's finally given up, and no one can blame him."

I was saddened by her words — saddened because I fully understood the unbearable agony Bill had suffered for six years.

I had endured that same agony as the slowest learner throughout my grade-school years.

And I was afraid — afraid Bill might have lost forever a good feeling about himself, that precious but fragile self-image that probably would tip the balance toward success and away from failure in later years.

That night, when we had our usual private moments together as I was "putting him to bed," I told him for the first time about my own grade-school experiences. I told him that some thirty years before I had been the dumbest kid in my class but, with the help of the love and understanding of my mother, father, and teachers, I somehow stumbled through those years and ultimately went on to law school.

I also told Bill it was easy to look at the achievements of others and think that they came simply and easily. But life usually is not that kind. Most of the good things that have happened to me and to others have grown out of the ashes of defeat and failure. Most of us have struggled mightily, suffered hundreds of agonizing defeats, and gone on to ultimate victory. Some have struggled with school, some with physical handicap, and others with the loss of a loved one. Almost every one of us has suffered and overcome defeats — and I believed Bill could and would also.

As I left Bill's bedroom after our nightly prayers, I turned to him and said, "Bill, I know that someday, in some way, you will become the greatest Leenhouts of them all."

"You know, Dad," he answered, "I guess that not doing so good isn't all that bad if someone loves you and stands by you."

So together we worked to turn this defeat into victory. With the help of Jim Roe, an eye doctor who developed perceptual, tactile, and motor coordination exercises to assist Bill's perception and coordination, and a special reading tutor who helped him with comprehension, Bill slowly progressed.

And Bill gave it his all. Each night immediately after dinner, his mother or I would accompany Bill to the basement where, with proper eye movements, he would follow the path our fingers traced around a bent coat-hanger circle or the motion of a ball swinging from side to side on a string. Then he would seclude himself in his upstairs bedroom and study, study, study until bedtime. Dr. Roe was amazed by — and greatly admired — Bill's determination to correct his physical handicap.

To everyone's amazement, Bill made the honor roll throughout junior high school and continued to maintain just under a B average through his senior year in high school. He did not accomplish this on native mental ability — he accomplished it almost solely on *desire*, that immeasurable, somewhat magical strength of a man's heart and soul that so often turns defeat into victory.

Bill's first attempts at football, baseball, and track were every bit as bad as his early performance in school. Being a non-achieving athlete myself who never made a varsity team, I must admit that he came by his athletic nonability honestly.

Despite our limited ability, both Bill and I loved to participate in sports. Since I really love kids and would rather be around them than anyone else, I enthusiastically volunteered to coach Bill's Flag Football team.

The young boys who choose to play football in our city, Royal Oak, Michigan, can play in either of two leagues. The kids who are the most gifted athletically, and who will probably go on to be varsity athletes, usually play Little League Football. The teams in this league play tough, hard, serious football, and considerable emphasis is placed on winning.

Those who are not so athletically gifted usually play Flag Football, a toned-down version of the game which resembles Touch Football more than Tackle. Each player attaches a small flag to his belt, and the opposition "tackles" the ball carrier simply by pulling off his flag. The philosophy for most of the coaches in this league is simple: "Let everyone play and have fun."

When Bill was eight we joined the nonachievers, the Flag Football League. We felt at home there for these were "our kinds of kids."

As the coach, I was determined to let every boy on our team play in every game in the hopes that these otherwise non-achievers in athletics might gain a feeling of accomplishment and develop a good self-image. I didn't really care if we won or lost. In fact, I hoped we might lose some games so the boys could learn how to handle losing as well as winning.

But despite the fact that everyone played, we won *every* game that first year, usually by a big score. Several boys on our team were fast and skillful enough to have played in the Little League. Yet they chose to play with us and we just couldn't lose, though I often shuffled the boys to each and every position. And Bill? He was awful. Most of the time he really didn't know, or really care, which way we were running the ball or even who had won. At the end of the game I would feel an inner hurt as one skinny, dirty little boy shuffled forlornly off the field and watched the rest of his teammates run off together for an afternoon of play. But when he reached me he would smile and reach out his little hand, and we would leave for another Saturday afternoon together.

Mainly to please me, I think, Bill stuck with Flag Football, and for four years I played him at center where he could do the least damage to the team. I told *him*, though — time and time again until I'm sure he believed it — that he was the center because he was the *one* guy I could rely upon always to start the play by hiking the ball to the correct player.

Thus Bill began to gain a feeling of achievement and accomplishment even though it was unearned. We all need to achieve, to accomplish, and to feel good about ourselves. When we are unable to earn it, someone has to love us enough to give us that feeling in such a way that we think we have earned it.

Without knowing it, I had learned this thirty years earlier when I was in the sixth grade. I was the slowest learner in the class and had a deplorable self-image. I didn't think I was, or ever would be, good for anything. But my sixth-grade teacher understood my problems and, more importantly, really loved me. She made sure I was one of the boys chosen to be a corner crossing guard. A crossing guard! Suddenly I felt important and useful. I *was* good for something after all. Someone had made me feel important, and I tried to do the same for our son.

Thus for four years Bill, thinking he was the most important boy on the team, centered the ball and stayed out of the way. During the last year of Flag Football he finally had his moment.

He played defensive halfback and intercepted a pass and ran it back for a touchdown. It was a small feat, perhaps, compared with the accomplishments of other players, but nonetheless his moment. Even then, victory was tainted. The team was ahead by seven touchdowns. I was playing everyone everywhere, trying to keep down the score and let the other team score. In the spring of Bill's first year of junior high, he tried out for the school baseball team. Bill worked hard and never missed a practice. But winning was such an important consideration that the coach let Bill play in only *two* games — in the late innings and in the outfield where the opposing hitters were least likely to hit the ball. The coach didn't let him bat, not even once all year.

I often wonder if the coach, the players, the students, the fans — or anyone else who had anything to do with the team of thirteen- and fourteen-year-old boys — now remember what the won-lost record was that year. Somebody *must* remember, because it was so important to win then that one kid, who never missed a practice, could not bat once.

Some adults wonder why many youngsters grow up with a distorted set of values. It is no wonder at all. Such youngsters learn early that victory, championships, status, prestige, and outward show seem to be the most important values of adult life.

A nearby high-school athletic team, for example, was outstanding in three consecutive years recently — a highly successful sports program. Yet some of us consider it one of the city's most unsuccessful sports because only about fifteen young men out of each class of about eight hundred students get to play. The competition for a position on the team is so deadly serious that many freshman boys who are cut from the team literally throw their spikes in disgust and despair into a dark basement corner and never pick them up again.

On the other hand, an "unsuccessful" high-school team in the area which struggles to win any of its games, let alone a championship, cuts no one from the freshman and sophomore teams. Every boy plays. Every young man in that school who is willing to attend practice faithfully and work hard experiences the thrill of making the freshman and junior varsity teams. Over the years, hundreds of young men who played in the "unsuccessful" program have experienced success, achievement, and self-esteem by being involved with an inspirational personality, the coach, in a wholesome activity. This to me is so much more important than the prestige of winning.

Bill decided he didn't care to try out again for a sport where so much emphasis was placed on winning and prestige, a sport where — no matter how hard he worked — he probably wouldn't get to bat once all year. So in the eighth grade he went out for track, a sport in which no one ever is cut from the team.

Jim Conley, the junior-high-school track coach, somehow ran every boy who was out for track in every meet. He usually ran slower boys like Bill in the relays and even in a few individual races when he could — but *every* boy ran in every meet.

During his first track season Bill lost every race badly. He never came close to winning. But with every defeat Bill seemed to grow more determined and worked even harder at achieving victory. Defeat didn't seem to bother him very much. Perhaps because he had suffered so many in his life, the probability or even certainty of a hundred more defeats just didn't seem that awesome or devastating.

One of Bill's friends, a boy who had been the fastest runner in our Flag Football League, also went out for junior-high-school track and easily won every race he ran in his first year. The next year, however, he lost one or two races; during his freshman season in senior high he lost regularly. But having been raised on victories, he could not comprehend or accept defeat and dejectedly gave up and quit the team. Early victories had paved the way for ultimate defeat.

Bill kept at it steadily. He ran with the freshman cross-country team the next fall and again finished poorly all year. At the end of the cross-country season Royal Oak's two high schools held a freshman meet. Bill ran as hard as he possibly could, as he always did, and near the end of the race was in fifth place about a quarter of a mile behind the leader. It looked as if he would end his season with another defeat.

Suddenly another runner challenged Bill from behind and, in his anxiety, elbowed and pushed Bill. Bill reacted as he never had before — he pushed back, ran harder, and held on to finish fifth. He had never before shown that kind of competitiveness in any sport. He hadn't cared who won our Flag Football games. He had never pushed back when he got pushed in his track meets. He had always worked very hard, and his desire was almost overwhelming at times. But his attitude toward other athletes, when they jostled and pushed him, had seemed to be, "If winning is that important to you, go ahead. I really don't care one way or the other."

The following winter months were filled with hope and encouragement as our talks together dwelled on one subject — not Bill's distant fifth-place finish out of eight runners, but his new spirit of competitiveness.

The high-school cross-country team's captain and top runner, Phil Ceeley, also had taken notice of Bill's intense desire and new found competitiveness and helped Bill develop further as a runner. Phil, who later received the Kimball High School trophy for outstanding achievement in athletics and academics, showed Bill the five-, ten-, and fifteen-mile training courses he had used to develop the toughness and endurance that helped him win All-State cross-country honors. Phil's training routes became Bill's training routes. And winning the All-State honors, as Phil had done, became Bill's goal.

How Bill worked at attaining that goal! He became a familiar figure on Royal Oak's streets, running five-to-fifteen miles a day — every day — through the snow, sleet, and bitter cold of winter, the driving, drenching rains of spring, and the sultry heat of summer.

A statement by Jim Ryun, the great miler from Kansas, spurred Bill during the dead of winter to develop toughness both physically and mentally. "It seems strange," Ryun said, "but I think the cold winters of Kansas gave me the toughness that I needed."

Like Phil, to relieve the monotony of seeing the same streets over and over, Bill tacked up a map of the United States on the basement wall and imagined himself running westward across the country. Periodically he would draw a line along the map's highways to record the number of miles he had run and, after three high school years of running, the black line weaved its way from Detroit to Los Angeles and halfway back.

But Bill continued to lose almost every race he ran until his senior year, when his desire and thousands of miles of hard work began to pay off. He became his high-school cross-country team's fastest runner; his teammates elected him a co-captain.

Still his goal of being All-State seemed unattainable. To achieve his ultimate dream he would have to beat literally thousands of runners, most with more natural athletic ability than he, in a Regional and finally a State meet. *Impossible*, I had thought before he and his team placed high enough in their Regional to run in this race, the Michigan State High School Cross-Country finals. And because he had defied all probability and overcome whelming odds to get even this one last chance at achieving his goal, again I had to think, *Impossible*. This would be another defeat — perhaps a final, crushing blow. He had climbed much farther than the others to reach his pinnacle — he would have an even longer way to fall.

Bill and I had talked of the impossible, as in the life of Glenn Cunningham, the great miler of the 1930s. Glenn as a small boy was severely burned when he and his brother were building a fire in the schoolhouse furnace. For many days it looked as if the useless legs would have to be amputated. But Glenn begged and pleaded so strongly that his parents delayed the amputation for a while. Yet, the doctors said Glenn not only would never run again, he would not even walk.

Days, months, then years of torturous effort followed. First came that day of just standing for a second and collapsing back into bed. Then that first step. Finally a second, then a third step. One day he walked again on legs that, according to the doctors, simply could not hold his weight. Further progress: his first jogging step. Then finally, running.

Gradually getting stronger and stronger, Glenn Cunningham — despite scar tissue, lack of arch support, and some missing toes — began to win races in high school. He went on to college and eventually set a world record for the mile in 1934. Others have come along now who have beaten Cunningham's time. None has beaten his legacy of courage and just plain "guts."

CRACK! THE STARTER'S GUN AGAIN SIGNALED THE beginning of an intense sixteen-minute drama. No second gun. No false start. This was it.

Bill and his rivals began their lonely, painful three-mile journey over hills, through forests, and "cross country." My heart was in my throat; my knees were weak. Bill seemed to be in bad position and hemmed in already. A husky voice left my throat and the chilly November winds carried my shouts of "Go Billy Blue!" to our son who wore the blue of Royal Oak Kimball High School.

I hurried along with some of the other spectators to a flat 150-yard stretch at the bottom of a hill near the quarter-mile mark, where we could next glimpse the runners. My 47-year-old legs would not move as fast as my heart wanted them to, but I reached the vantage point as the first runner burst into view. I strained my eyes and, though I couldn't see his face, could tell by the runner's style that it was not Bill. Every runner has his distinct, recognizable manner of running.

Two, three, four more runners came into view. *Five, six, seven — where is he?* For a moment I was struck by the sickening thought that perhaps Bill was forced to drop out. He had never quit a race, no matter how badly he was running or how far behind he fell. But there was always the first time — there was always a chance of a severe charley horse or stomach cramps.

Eight, nine, ten and still no sign of Bill. Thirty-three . . . thirty-six . . . thirty-nine . . . there he is, erect, his right shoulder lurching up and down with each pumping motion of his loosely swinging arms. The stride is unmistakable. My heart sank, for there were thirty-nine runners ahead of him. And even before I could see his facial features I knew Bill was working hard — too hard. When he won the league meet a few weeks before, he seemed at times to glide effortlessly along the ground. Not now. Now he seemed to be pressing, pushing. Every muscle was forcing and straining.

I wished he could stop and tell me, "I feel fine, Dad," or "My stomach is cramped," or "My legs feel heavy." Another runner hemmed him in on the inside. As Bill got a little closer,

I could see his face already racked with pain.

Suddenly Bill moved to the outside and began to pass some runners. He knew, and so did I, that he could not afford to fall very far behind, for he did not have a "kick," a great burst of speed, that he could rely on at the end of the race. He gained momentum and, as he passed me, raised his clenched right fist just a little as if to tell me he was okay.

"Go Blue!" I yelled to encourage all our team's runners. But deep in my heart I knew who Blue was — "Billy Blue." Bill had picked up this nickname from a teammate when he first made varsity as a sophomore.

As he swept by, he continued to pass the runners ahead of him. And if the determined look on his face mirrored his thoughts, he was thinking, *Man, there's no way I'm going to louse this up.*

Could his desire and our love carry him over the remaining miles to the victory he dreamed of? It seemed impossible. "Go Blue!" I hollered as he disappeared over the next hill.

II
Taking Time to Share

WHENEVER I MEET A NEW FATHER, AGLOW WITH biological triumph, I have an urge to say, "Just wait. There's more to being a father than you think." But I don't say it, for he may turn out to be one of those fellows with a natural instinct for fatherhood, a talent that I have concluded is as rare as perfect pitch. For most of us, fatherhood, like everything else worthwhile, requires work — lots of hard work. True, it is a labor of love, but labor nevertheless.

I made the decision easily and early to put a high priority on fatherhood and to work hard at it. But I had to learn *how* to be a father the hard way, and only a patient wife and a trio of charitable sons turned me into any kind of a parent at all.

Me, a father? Incredible! I thought to myself after my bride of a few months had whispered into my ear, "I think we're going to have a baby." Bursting with pride, I must have stood in front of the mirror for fifteen minutes the next morning, congratulating the face filled with amazement and disbelief that grinned back at me. *Wow, I did it! I didn't know I had it in me!*

The months flashed by, and our first baby was born prematurely on an unusually cold Fourth of July weekend. My wife's pain and my concern quickly gave way to relief — two arms, two legs, enough fingers and toes — then to joy. A son!

What a thrilling thing to happen to an ordinary guy like me! His mother, my wife, exhausted and nearly as white as the sheets she lay upon, looked more beautiful than ever. At that moment our whole life was rolled up into one little six-pound, helpless collection of skin and bones.

The big day came when I brought them home to our little apartment and my wife handed our son to me to carry upstairs. I wasn't really prepared for her request and gave her a fearful "couldn't you do it?" look. But she shook her head and said, to reassure me and perhaps herself, "Don't be afraid of him, silly, he won't break."

So, as my shaking hands clutched at the squirming little body somewhere in that blue blanket, I suspected that fatherhood, rather than one uninterrupted joy after another, was more likely to be a duty, an obligation.

A few days later, long before I was ready to rise one morning, my suspicions were confirmed. Bill started to cry. It was feeding time. I thought my wife must have overslept, so I turned over and closed my eyes again. The wailing from the living room-nursery went up a decibel or two. My wife was faking, I decided. But I couldn't just roll over and shout, "Go feed our child." She might reply, "Why don't you?" Then what would I say?

I puzzled about it for a minute while the crying continued, until I realized that if my wife *were* faking, she wouldn't admit it. So I could get up and feed Bill without establishing a precedent.

It was an awkward business. Fumbling around like the sorcerer's apprentice, I sterilized, measured, and capped in great clouds of steam. I tried unsuccessfully to quiet Bill while the bottle warmed. The nipple was clogged, the bottle got too hot, and there seemed to be no comfortable way to hold him. Finally we reached an accommodation and he sucked away. It wasn't all that bad.

Yet, though I confess I felt a certain pride in eliciting a hearty burp from him when the operation was over, I looked upon the whole affair as an immense obligation I wished I need never repeat — a wish that was not to be granted.

The obligations grew with Bill, and shortly after his fourth birthday, I was pressed into service as a disciplinarian. Although

I had aspired to be — as Carl Sandburg expressed it of Lincoln* — "both steel and velvet, who is as hard as rock and soft as drifting fog," my debut as a disciplinarian was a flop.

I was working in the garage when the little neighbor girl Bill had been playing with ran past the open door crying, "Billy hit me! Billy hit me!" Being a member of the old school that believes you shouldn't hit girls no matter how great the provocation, I grabbed a nearby board and rushed angrily to the backyard where Bill, evidently unaware of the dastardly deed he had just committed, still played happily with his toy dump truck. I hoisted him by his shirt collar and, while administering a lecture about courtesy to females, whacked him on his posterior with the board.

As he ran wailing into the garage and clutching the seat of his pants, my wife emerged quickly from the house and, arms folded tightly across her chest, asked sternly, "Why did you spank him? Did you see what happened?"

"Well, uh, not exactly," I replied sheepishly, "but the neighbor girl said Bill hit her."

"That's a terrible way for a lawyer to act," she continued. "You punished without finding out the facts. That little girl has been bothering Bill for a long time, and Billy kept trying to get her to leave him alone. So finally he pushed her, *very gently*, just to let her know he didn't want her that close to him. He certainly didn't hit her. He really couldn't have handled the situation any differently or any better."

Ashamed, I shifted my eyes from my wife's cold stare. Searching for an inviting spot on the ground to stare at, I noticed the tip of a rusty nail sticking out of the board with which I had just swatted Bill. I rushed into the garage. Just as I feared, the spot on Bill's little derriere that he was rubbing so vigorously

*Sandburg offered the explanation that Lincoln was hard in commanding a terrible civil war, in requiring subscription of soldiers for the first time in America, for suspending the right of habeas corpus. Yet he was soft, as indicated by his letter to the widow Mrs. Bixby (21 November 1864) and by his commitment to the postwar South: "With malice toward none, with charity for all." These remarks were made by Sandburg before a Joint Session of Congress and the assembled diplomatic corps on 12 February 1959.

had been slightly punctured by the nail.

Half an hour later, after giving Bill a preventative tetanus shot, the doctor asked, "By the way, how did this happen, Keith?" Happily he was a friend who accepted and did not try to refute my terse reply, "None of your business."

After that experience I decided never again to touch Bill in anger. As it turned out, I didn't have to. All I had to do is express disapproval, by facial expressions or in words, and that proved to be punishment enough.

Another year of duties, obligations, and sacrifices passed. Instead of going to Friday-night high-school football games with my friends, Bill and I stood on the railroad tracks overlooking the gridiron where I spent half my time watching him build imaginary fires and half my time watching the game. I gave up golf to spend Saturday and Sunday afternoons with him. And I tried not to stay up so late on weekend nights that I would be too tired the next day to play with him.

I accepted all these sacrifices and more, not because I particularly wanted to, but because I felt I should. This never truly bothered me, however, for I had always believed that true happiness is found in the fulfillment of duties, not in the pursuit of joys.

Then, on a bitterly cold January day when Bill was five, I unexpectedly discovered that fatherhood is not duties, obligations, and sacrifices, but a great joy. That entire Saturday afternoon I tried to help Bill learn to use single-bladed skates on a neighbor's frozen backyard swimming pool.

All afternoon Bill tried and failed to skate the full length of the pool. Finally, with red cheeks taut with determination, and with staccato puffs of steamy breath shooting through the wool scarf that covered his mouth, he skated all the way across. He made it!

Well, I should say, part of him made it. Just before he reached his goal, the end of the pool, he tripped and smacked his nose on the edge. I skated over, picked him up, and said elatedly, "You made it, Bill! That was really great!"

But rubbing his nose and looking at the bright red blood

staining the snow on his mittens, he looked up at me through his tears and sniffed, "I-I didn't think it was so great."

I began to laugh, not so much because of what he had said and done, but because suddenly, standing there on my ice skates, wiping blood from the nose of our five-year-old son, I realized I was with Bill because I loved him and would rather be with him than with anyone else in the entire world, except of course his mother.

What a beautiful moment! I no longer felt I was "giving up something." I was receiving an experience of myself that had released a new potential for loving. Fatherhood was no longer just a duty — it had just become one of the greatest experiences I would ever know.

My "job" of putting Bill to bed at night became my joy. My wife had him all day, so I wanted him for at least part of the evening. Each night as I put him to bed, we had fifteen minutes or so all alone, behind closed doors, away from everyone else. I came to look upon those fifteen minutes with Bill — and later with his two brothers — as just about the greatest moments of my day.

We spent most of that time talking about a very important subject — *nothing*. We usually mentioned whatever happened to be at the top of our heads or hearts at the moment. Sometimes we talked about the best and the worst things that happened to us that day. Or perhaps about great men and women we both knew. Gordie Howe, Al Kaline, and the University of Michigan football team were all great topics for nothing-conversations. We finished our talks by telling "Jesus stories" and saying our prayers together.

One evening, typical of many during my ten years as judge of our city's municipal court, a mother called and asked me to speak at her PTA meeting.

"How late can I come and still accommodate you?" I asked.

"You can speak at about nine o'clock after we conduct our business meeting if you like," she replied. "Why? Do you have some other important business to attend to?"

"Yes," I answered. "I'd like to put our sons to bed before I leave."

"*You* put your kids to bed!" she replied in amazement. "I can't believe it! My husband has never put our kids to bed — not once. He's too busy reading his newspaper."

Her reply and the dozens of others like it that I heard over the years bewildered me. I couldn't understand why so many fathers were preoccupied. Why couldn't they find the time to participate in the lives of their sons and daughters?

Unfortunately it usually wasn't simply a case of fathers shunning an area of responsibility they felt traditionally belonged to their wives; I was also amazed at how few fathers participated with their sons in traditionally male sports activities. Our Flag Football team, for example, played every Saturday for three months; though there were twenty boys on the team, only two or three fathers came to any games, and then usually only one or two games.

After a game in which they had played particularly well, I asked two brothers — one a fast halfback and the other an end who caught most of our passes — where their Dad was. I could hardly believe their answer: "Oh, he likes to sleep late on Saturday mornings and usually stays in bed until noon."

Another team member, Gary, was not a good player and usually handed off to the faster runners all game long. But late in the fourth period of one very close contest, we called a special play. Gary faked a handoff, kept the ball, and ran sixty yards up the middle for a touchdown to tie the score. We held the other team on downs and got the ball again with only a few seconds to go. Again we called the play, and Gary ran up the middle for a second touchdown. We won, and Gary's teammates swarmed him! It was the kind of moment I wish every boy and his father could share at least once.

But Gary's father wasn't there. A few days later I saw him and told him about his son's game-winning touchdowns.

"Gee, that's funny," he said. "Gary didn't tell me about it. I wonder why?"

"Why weren't you at the game to *see* his great moment?" I blurted without thinking.

"Oh, I had some work to do around the house," he replied.

I shouldn't have done it, I suppose, but I did: "Maybe if you had watched your son play once, he would have told you about his great moment," I told him.

Bill's youngest brother, Jim, played on the hockey team. As I watched game after game, I noticed that most of the other fathers weren't there. I asked one friend why he didn't come to watch his son play. "Oh, I really don't care too much for hockey," he explained.

Doesn't he know that you don't go to your son's games to see hockey? I thought. *If you want to watch hockey, you go to see the Detroit Red Wings play. Here you go to watch your son, not hockey.*

Where have all the fathers gone? Why do we put so many things before fatherhood? Why do we work around the house, at our jobs, at our golf games, at everything but fatherhood?

Perhaps it's because today we fathers are often uncertain about our role. We feel inadequate and then guilty. We are torn, many of us, between our interest in our children and a driving concern for our jobs; our society has made us feel apologetic about that conflict by labeling us "absentee fathers." And as we are blamed, whether justly or unjustly, for defection from a role that is at best no longer clear-cut, we begin to substitute other, apparently more satisfying, activities for those of fathering.

But there needn't be this conflict between children and work. A man shouldn't have to decide to devote both the quantity and quality of his time to one to the neglect and exclusion of the other. As a friend of mine put it so well, "I believe that both the quality of time you spend *with* your children and the quality of time you spend *away* from them is much more important than the quantity. If you have to spend time away from home, make sure it's *quality* time. Your family will know and understand that you are away for a good reason. But they'll also know if you are gone just because you don't want to be home with them.

"And when you are home, really spend *quality* time with your children. It's better to give them your absolute, undivided attention for five hours a week than to be with them thirty hours a week, too engrossed in your newspaper even to talk to them."

My friend lived his philosophy well. When he was home he spent quality time with his children until they went to bed. When he was gone, his children knew he was spending quality time serving his community by heading up a needed youth program.

When Bill was still very young, I traveled to St. Louis for an important meeting. While there, I visited a Methodist settlement house for underprivileged children. This visit perhaps more than any other experience of my life graphically convinced me of the extreme importance of spending quality time with children. I had handled many cases reflecting child-neglect in my years on the bench, but nothing could have prepared me for what I heard.

"We teach religion here," said the house manager, a gray-haired Methodist minister who hoped and loved many for whom hope and love was not found elsewhere. "But we have to teach it quite a bit differently than you might be used to. How many times have you heard or said, 'God is like a father' or 'God the Father'? Well, we can't tell these children that God is like a father, because each kid here has been beaten, abused, sworn at, screamed at, and spit upon by his father, usually an alcoholic who eventually has deserted his children and home. If we tell these kids that God is like a father, they will have nothing at all to do with God.

"The sad fact is that each kid thinks there is something wrong with him," the manager continued. "They often say, usually to themselves but sometimes out loud, 'What's wrong with me? Other kids have dads who don't beat them and leave them. What's wrong with *me*?' We know there is something wrong, of course — with the father, not the child. But the kids don't know that."

His words cut through my heart like a hot knife blade. If I had needed a driving force, I now had one. I *had* to work hard at being a good father so that when Bill and his brothers heard that God is like a father, they would want to be with God now and always.

But our father-son relationship did not become a one-sided affair with me doing all the giving and Bill all the receiving. Bill's influence on me was profound and far-reaching.

Bill's first great effect on me was in the form of a gift — a new and full realization of what love and sacrifice mean. When Bill was a baby, I often sacrificed my early morning sleep to quiet his piercing hungry cry with a bottle. As I sleepily held our contented infant son, both of us surrounded by an over-stuffed armchair and bathed in the soft, shadowy-red, predawn light, I began to fathom the unspoken, sometimes stern, but deep fatherly love that had been poured into me as a child.

I finally understood and, more importantly, could tell and show my father how much I appreciated the sacrifices he had made for me, how grateful I was to him, and how deep was my love for him. But my father knew of my complete gratitude and love for him for only a few months. He died when Bill was six months old. I owe to Bill those six short months and the ability to express my love for my father as never before. Only Bill could have bestowed such a great gift on me.

In the ensuing years, while I struggled as a young lawyer to give Bill economic security, I again thought of my father and the unmentioned sacrifices he must have made for me. I was four when our country was engulfed by the Great Depression and about fourteen when it finally ended. Most of my con-temporaries have intense, unpleasant memories of that era. But though my dad earned only about $900 a year as a bank trust officer, he made me feel completely secure; I never was aware of the heavy burdens and worries that at times must have nearly crushed his mind and spirit.

As the burdens that accompanied a law practice and later a judgeship grew upon my heart and mind, I discovered that Bill had an almost magical effect on me. One night as I pulled a thick homemade quilt under his chin and tucked it over his bony little shoulders, I paraphrased for him a poem I had once read and long remembered.

"Sometimes things just don't go right for me, Bill," I said. "And somehow it seems that those you have loved the most and have tried to help out the most just don't seem to understand. When this happens I come home feeling pretty bad, discouraged, and blue. Then something amazing happens. A little man suddenly appears. He is sort of dirty, has a runny nose, and sometimes he has not behaved as well as he should have during the day. And it seems like I start picking up his playthings from the time I step out of the car until I reach the front door.

"So there I stand, tired, discouraged, and hurt in the heart, and suddenly that little man makes me feel better by saying just two magical words — 'Hi, dad.' Bill, that little man who has that magical power is you."

This was one of the first really meaningful conversations we ever had. By it Bill discovered that our relationship did not all consist in my giving and his receiving. He was giving also. For him, as for the rest of us human kind, one of the real joys of life is in giving. Bill felt this joy that night and, I believe, has been quietly proud of what he has given me ever since.

In 1969, after spending ten years as the judge of our city's municipal court, I resigned. I did this largely for one reason — Bill. I had promised myself, when I was first elected and Bill was only four years old, that I would not be the judge of our city court when he entered high school. I thought that Bill, as a shy teenager and struggling student and athlete, would already be at an uncomfortable time of life; being labeled "the judge's son" would be an additional, undesirable pressure. So when Bill was halfway through the eighth grade, I decided to resign, a decision I have never regretted, looking through either his eyes or mine.

Bill also influenced the way I invested what little money I could. I started to invest modestly in real estate; I made this choice as opposed to other forms of investment so that Bill and later his brothers could appreciate our investment by actually experiencing it. When he skated on the frozen lake in the winter, swam in it during the summer, and explored the property while playing, it meant something to him and he understood that it was ours. How could he have experienced and how could I have explained to him ownership of municipal bonds, commodities, or stock certificates?

Bill influenced not only what I invested in, but also how. In 1966, for example, Van, my real estate partner, approached me with an interesting proposition. He had heard of a large, potentially valuable piece of vacant property soon to be placed on the market in a nearby fast-growing city.

Van took me to look at the land, and I liked the location, price, and potential. But as we were driving back to my office I asked him, "Will we buy this vacant land, hold onto it for a while, and then sell for whatever profit we can realize, as we've done on our other investments?"

"No, Keith," Van answered. "We'd have to develop this piece ourselves — you know, build apartments and stores, deal with contractors and subcontractors, and that sort of thing. But I'd need only twenty hours a week of your time to do it, Keith — I'll put in sixty hours a week. And believe me, when we're through, I have no doubts whatsoever that we'll each be a million or two richer."

Two million dollars — twenty hours a week! Two million dollars — twenty hours a week! Van's words echoed through my mind as I sat alone in my study later that evening. What should I do? Fifty-five to sixty hours of my time each week — time that could not be spared or shared — was taken up by the duties of my judgeship. The twenty hours a week would have to come from the time I spent with my family and teaching a high-school-age Sunday school class.

I made my decision. I called Van the next day and told him I couldn't get involved in a real estate venture that would take so much time away from my wife and sons, no matter how much money I could make. Van, as it turned out, was greatly relieved, for he had agonized over the same considerations and arrived at the same decision.

The people who bought the land did, in fact, make several million dollars. But there is no doubt in my mind that we made the right decision.

Bill's influence on me never ceases to amaze me. I worked so hard at fatherhood, at first out of a sense of duty and then out of love. I tried so hard to consider what was best for Bill, not only for myself, in the decisions I made. I cannot *now* think of a single time that a decision based upon looking at the world through our son's eyes was not the correct decision for all of us.

III
And the Word Became Flesh

MANY OF US HAVE BEEN INFLUENCED BY OR HAVE patterned our lives after one passage of Scripture. The words that have prevailed upon my mind, heart, and soul for so many years appear in the first chapter of the Gospel of John. The writer's fingers must have trembled as he struggled to express the overwhelming truth revealed to him — *"And the Word became flesh and dwelt among us."*

How often I thought about those words. And the more I thought about them, the more I came to imagine a God who looked down from the heavens and became increasingly frustrated by the fact that we did not comprehend His love for us. We did not understand, and we did not respond.

He had given His laws. He even numbered them for us, one through ten, but we still didn't understand. Through His prophets He sent more words, but we still did not comprehend the full meaning of His love.

God must have realized, perhaps even suddenly, that we would never understand His redemptive love by communicating to us with words, laws, rules, and commandments. We simply do not understand them because *we* are not words, laws, rules and commandments. He had to wrap up His message of love for us in the personality of Christ.

When that personality bled, we understood because we bleed. When He was lonely, deserted, betrayed, denied, when He suffered and died, we understood because we are lonely, deserted, betrayed and denied, and we suffer and die. When the love of God became flesh in the personality of Christ, His redemptive process of love culminated.

When I took the bench in the Municipal Court of Royal Oak, Michigan, in 1959, I faced a situation that was similarly frustrating. Most of the offenders who stood before me did not comprehend the meaning of our laws, statutes, and commandments and, as a result, our decrees and punishments rarely succeeded in rehabilitating them. They needed to be *shown* a better way to live.

As the judge, all I could do was look at these defendants for a few seconds after they were found guilty or pleaded guilty and say, "You pay a fine" or "You go to jail" or both. Nothing else. Like cattle that file through stockyards one by one and are killed by a quick blow on the head as quickly as they appear, so we would fine and jail offenders, without thought or hesitation, one after the other, all day long, day after day, month after month, year after year.

Here was all this need, and all we did in the court was blindly punish the defendant. He might be a deserted, lonely, and emotionally beaten teenager. Fine and jail! He might be an alcoholic, alone and terribly sick. Fine and jail! He might have had a quarrel with his wife and, out of anger, hit someone though he had never done it before. Fine and jail! He might be emotionally ill. Fine and jail!

We were tough. We knew just what to do. Punish! Punish! Punish!

And, God forgive us, we were stupid. So many came back again and again and again. We were supposed to help solve these offenders' problems and make our streets safer. But in many, many cases we created more problems and made our streets less safe by adding bitterness, hostility, and aggressiveness to a lifetime of already seemingly insurmountable problems. They had hurt society, so society, through the court, punished and hurt them back. Then they wanted to hurt society even more severely, so society in return hurt them even more severely until one sad fact became clearly established. Eighty-five percent or more of those who eventually committed our most serious crimes (felonies like murder, rape, and armed robbery) first committed a less serious crime — a misdemeanor like shoplifting, drunkenness, or fighting — and appeared before a lower court judge like me.

Think of it! Eighty-five percent of our worst criminals appeared before courts as young, minor offenders years before they committed their serious acts of crime. And we treated them without pity. They learned well — their later acts of serious crime were often without pity.

We had to change the system, and we did. We wrapped up the concern we had in our hearts for the offender in the form of an inspiring personality — volunteer citizens from our community. Jews, Christians, atheists, men, women, blacks, whites, young college students, retirees — people who cared involved themselves on a one-to-one basis with our offenders and showed them, through their own examples, a better way to live. Then the offender understood, because the concern of the court became flesh and blood. The word of law became flesh in the inspiring volunteer personality. This, then, was the beginning of a rehabilitative process that has succeeded time and again.

It took fifteen to twenty hours a week over and above the forty hours a week I worked as the judge, for ten long years. Yet my contribution was rather insignificant compared with others. Hundreds of volunteers donated more than 50,000 hours a year so we could first analyze each offender's problems and then provide the combination of discipline and treatment which fit each one's unique needs. Carefully conducted research proved that our rate of repeat crime was reduced by some 75 percent as compared with another, similar court that did not use volunteers.*

*For the complete story of this research and the once-unique, now-widespread rehabilitative program, see *First Offender* by Joe Alex Morris, published by Funk and Wagnalls, available from Volunteers in Probation, 200 Washington Square Plaza, Royal Oak, Michigan 48067. Information about using volunteers in courts, prisons, jails, and juvenile institutions may also be obtained from the V.I.P. office.

We began in 1959. Fourteen years later some 300,000 citizen-volunteers were involved with offenders in some two thousand courts, jails, prisons, and juvenile institutions across the country. The word of law has truly become flesh.

Bill and I discussed the concept of the "word becoming flesh" many times in our sauna, at bedtime, and in the high-school Sunday School class I taught. We decided that because of the paradoxical nature of Christ, the concept of God's rules and commandments becoming flesh was not such a simple and easy concept to understand.

We should be humble because certainly Christ was humble. When He was called good, He protested, "Why call Me good? No one is good but God." Yet on another occasion he said, "I am the Way, the Truth, and the Life. There is no other way to heaven but Me." Humble? Or an egomaniac? Or both?

We should be gentle because Christ was gentle. "Gentle Jesus meek and mild, Look upon a little child," we have sung for generations. "Turn the other cheek," Christ Himself said. Yet He drove the moneychangers out of the temple with a fierceness and bold courage which has been rarely matched. Gentle? Or a man of fierce courage and bold action? Or both?

We should be forgiving because He was forgiving. On the cross He cried out, "Forgive them, Father, for they know not what they do." On another occasion He told His disciples to forgive "seventy times seven," meaning without limit. Yet He also said that he who harmed a child would be better off had he never been born. Or he would be better off if a millstone were tied around his neck and he were cast into the depths of the sea. Forgiving? Or unforgiving? Or both?

In our six-by-six-foot sauna, our Finnish steam bath — our bodies wet with perspiration, sweat smarting our eyes, and faces glowing red in the two-hundred-plus-degree heat — we talked and pondered the mysteries of the life of Christ. Only by study, thought, and prayer could the apparent contradictions and paradoxes be resolved. Only by study, thought, and prayer could we know Him.

We also talked about religion, God, and the life of Christ during the many wilderness canoe trips we took together. The first trip I remember taking with Bill was into the exclusive wilderness area in northern Minnesota and Canada when he was only four years old. No roads wind their way through this virgin forest land. Airplanes are banned. The air belongs only to the clouds, gulls, and soft singing breezes. We can invade the hundreds of crystal blue lakes only by alternately paddling and portaging our canoe and meager supplies.

One star-filled evening, with the water lapping on our island, the forlorn sound of the crying loons echoing across the water, and the flickering of the dying fire casting dancing shadows on our tent, I explained to Bill the temptations Jesus experienced in the wilderness after His baptism.

Concluding, I asked Bill what would have happened had Jesus used His great power for His own selfish purposes — for food, health, or power. Bill thought seriously for a few moments, then answered, "If Jesus had used those powers for His own self, Dad, God would have taken all His powers away." What a great insight from our four-year-old son! What a thrilling moment for me! We were to share many such moments.

Years later, on another wilderness adventure, we carefully placed a burning candle on a rock at our shore campsite and left for an evening of surface-casting for bass. It was so dark when we returned that I could barely see young Bill silently paddling in the front of the canoe. But over two miles away we could see our candle, a beacon glowing brightly in the dark. The night was so still that the candle barely flickered. We said our prayers as we paddled toward that beautiful candle, and I sang some hymns. We talked about love, life, Christ, and him and me during those beautiful two miles that were forever uniquely ours.

Yes, we talked some of religion, love, and our feelings for each other. But mostly, to the best of our ability, we *lived* love. We didn't have to talk about it, for the words *love for each other* based upon our love of the Lord became flesh. This we both understood.

To the best of my ability, I wrapped up my love for Bill in my heart, body, mind, and soul so that the word *love* truly became flesh. If Bill in and through my flesh — my body, my soul, my mind — could sense the love of God and give God his love, then I had done my job as a father. If not, I had failed. To me it was that simple.

An early indication that I had succeeded came when Bill and I were driving to a Sunday school weekend retreat during his freshman year in high school. As we looked at and talked about the beautiful star-filled night, I blurted, "Bill, we don't talk about it very much, but do you understand that in my life Christ is what it's all about?"

"Dad, it comes over loud and clear," he unhesitatingly replied.

I first really knew that my attempt to live love for Christ, rather than preach it to Bill, had succeeded at least a little when Bill was a sophomore. Somehow he had gained the seventh and last varsity spot on the cross-country team that fall. No one thought he would, and it was truly his first meaningful victory after a long string of defeats.

In a minor race run just before the important Regionals, the entire team finished poorly. Bill, as the seventh and last man, ran the slowest he had run all year. In the reserve meet, right after the varsity meet, a boy we will call "Steve" finished the race with a slightly faster time than Bill.

For the first time that year the coach had to choose who would run in the next race — the important Regionals: Bill or Steve. Steve had run faster than Bill in the previous meet, but Bill had run far more consistently all year. We all wondered what the coach's decision would be. I was concerned that, if the coach chose Steve, Bill would be deeply affected by another defeat — especially in its coming on the heels of his first taste of success.

On Friday Bill told us the coach had decided to run Steve. But Bill did not appear disappointed, and I wondered why. That night, in the sauna, Bill told me the entire story:

The whole team voted and selected Bill to run in the Regional meet. But after the meeting Bill went to the coach and said,

"Coach, I really think Steve should run. You see, if he doesn't, he might get discouraged and quit, and we need him on the team next year. Besides, I'll still be your friend whether I run or not. But if you don't let Steve run, he might not be friends with you anymore, and I really think Steve needs your friendship." I was overwhelmed and told Bill he had just performed a truly Christlike act. He simply replied, "Oh, I didn't think about that. I just did what I thought was best for Steve and for the team." I was very, very pleased, because our son was now instinctively developing a Christlike life.

The next Saturday Steve ran poorly and eventually quit the team. Bill ran in the reserve meet and won it easily with a much faster time than Steve had.

The night of the reserve meet, we talked for the first time about victory and how to handle success — not that Bill had handled his first triumph badly. On the contrary, he shook hands with the other runners after the race and trotted off by himself to "warm down" exactly as he had done through all the defeats.

For sixteen years we had talked only about how to handle defeat, and I guess it was a simple pleasure for both of us to talk for a change about the obligations that accompany victory.

We talked about Judge Arthur E. Moore, a former juvenile judge of our county. He was my Sunday school teacher in high school and did incredible things as a jurist back in the thirties and forties. He was fully three decades ahead of his time; many judges are only beginning to do now what he did then. He was, and is, my judicial ideal.

Years ago Judge Moore established "Camp Oakland." This facility enables delinquent kids to enjoy a beautiful farmlike home where they learn auto mechanics, farming, living together, discipline, and most of all, loving. Great things have happened on those acres.

When I first became a judge, Judge Moore told me, "Keith, if you do things differently, get ready to have a lot of mud thrown in your face." He said it with sincerity and sadness. He knew. He had a lot of mud thrown in his face because he loved kids — as no other judge I know of loved kids in the 1930s and 1940s.

He knew, and so did I, that I could not conceive of treating offenders who appeared before our court the way they had always been processed. Like cattle who come through the stockyards and are killed by being struck on the head, one after another as quickly as they appear, we would fine and jail the offenders, without hesitation, one after the other all day long, day after day.

It was incredible what we were doing. The process had to be changed, and there was only one way to do it. The volunteer power of the citizens in our city — the people who cared — had to become involved. We began. In October 1965 the *Reader's Digest* printed the first story about Royal Oak ("Royal Oak Aids Its Problem Youth"). It was to have a profound effect on the spread of the idea to a few other courts, then others, and by 1972 to some two thousand courts, jails, prisons, and juvenile institutions.

The article was to have a deepening effect in other ways also. In 1965 the National Association of Municipal Judges met in Montreal. This was the kickoff for Volunteers in Probation, a Division of the National Council on Crime and Delinquency, as our organization came to be known. Among other things, the Michigan judges met for a breakfast. Twenty-six of us were at the convention; only twenty-five were invited to the breakfast. Both Audrey and I felt bad about it. I had never had any quarrel or misunderstanding with any of them. But I had decided to do what had not been done before and, I guess, that is putting your head above the crowd.

"Bill," I told my son after the reserve meet, "as you win and become better and better, your head will get farther and farther over the crowd, and mud really hurts when it hits you in the face."

My fatherly instincts told me I had to help prepare him for victory and success as well as defeat and failure. Sometimes I think the first is even more difficult than the second.

I told Bill also about Boyd Rucket — a rugged, weathered farmer who worked the rolling, golden wheat fields of south-eastern Washington — about his handsome butterscotch-and-white collie-German shepherd, Buster, and about the unforgettable lesson in humility they taught me.

During the summer of 1950 Jerry Cohen and I drove truck for Boyd, taking wheat from his fields to a granary into nearby Pomeroy. Jerry and I were close, lifelong friends and that summer we were between our first two years of law school.

On a hot, dry afternoon as I was about to embark on another routine drive to the granary, Boyd ran over to the truck, his rough voice huffing, "Keith, ther're some cows in the field just south of our barn. After you drop this load off, take Buster, here, and get him to drive the cows back where they belong."

"Okay, Boyd," I agreed as Buster, a constant companion in the truck, leaped through the open window to his customary position beside me. We were great friends, and I almost thought of him as my dog.

After unloading the grain in town, Buster and I hurried back to Boyd's farmhouse. There we exchanged the rusting, old wooden-boxed truck for a new jeep and headed over the roadless field to the grazing cows. I hand-vaulted out of the topless jeep and, with Buster playfully nipping at my heels and shirtsleeves, jogged to the south of the cows.

"Buster," I commanded, "drive them back where they belong."

Deliberately Buster circled to the north of the cows and, ignoring my waving arms and my shouts, began driving them further south, away from Boyd's barn.

Buster was obviously pleased with himself and, expecting praise from me for a job well done, tried to nuzzle his nose under my tightly clenched fist. His wagging tail dropped as I angrily told him how stupid he was.

Again, further out in the field, I led Buster by his collar southward past the cows and told him, "This time do it right. Put the cows where they belong." But again Buster carefully picked his way through the cows until he was north of them. Again he drove them south, even further from Boyd's barn.

Sweat poured down my face, flushed now from heat and anger. I really wanted to give up but just couldn't let Boyd down, so we tried once more. This time Buster, ignoring all my pleas, screams, and threats, drove the bellowing herd over a hill, through a tiny creek, up a brushy embankment, and right up next to a weathered-gray, sway-backed barn which belonged to "Old Bill,'" a bachelor farmer and Boyd's nearest neighbor.

"One of us is stupid!" I gasped and screamed at Buster when I finally scrambled through the brush and reached the barn. And that's only a little bit of what I said. But Buster wasn't angry; he merely looked up at me with hurt in those beautiful brown eyes. We were such good friends, and he couldn't understand why I was so angry with him.

We sped back to Boyd's house, where I leaped from the jeep back into the truck. I slammed the door, started the motor, and began to pull away from the animal that had caused me so much trouble. Nevertheless, he looked so sad and forlorn that I relented, saying, as I opened the door, "Okay, come on, Buster. After all, you're only a stupid mongrel. I shouldn't expect so much from you, I guess."

When we got back to the fields, the buzzing anger in my head sank like a lead weight to the pit of my stomach as I suddenly realized that, not only had I failed to drive the cows back to Boyd's barn, but also I had committed the wheat truck driver's cardinal sin. Boyd's combine sat idly in the field with a full load of wheat. I was supposed to load "on the run," and the combine was not to stop except for lunch and repairs.

As I pulled the truck to a halt, Boyd ran over and shouted angrily, "Where in the world have you been, Keith?" Chagrined, I reported the whole story of how, despite all my efforts, Buster had driven the cows right next to Old Bill's barn.

Suddenly all the wind-, sun-, and time-etched cracks on Boyd's square, brown face turned upward into a great smile, then a howling laugh as he gasped, "What's wrong with that, Keith? Those are Old Bill's cows!"

I stared silently at my chaff- and dust-covered leather boots for a few seconds, then in humiliation shifted my glance to Buster. By placing his paws on my chest and licking my face with his tongue, he eagerly accepted the apology that filled my eyes.

"Buster, one of us is stupid." The words echoed in my mind. No doubt they were true, but they didn't apply to Buster. It was a humbling experience I have never forgotten.

Nine years later when I was elected judge, I discovered that sitting on the bench is not a particularly humbling process. Like the Roman centurion of old, I would say "Come" and they would come, "Go" and they would go. So under the glass that covered my desktop I slipped a quote from the Book of Micah with one slight addition: "What does the Lord require of you but to do justly, to love mercy, and to walk humbly with your God . . . and . . . *remember Buster."*

The memory of my experience with Buster helped me meet the difficult task of attaining and retaining some sense of humility while being what a judge is, a small god in his courtroom. Each day as I entered the courtroom, I uttered a short silent prayer for understanding, patience, and courage to make the right decision, be it punishment, treatment, or a combination of both. And I always ended the prayer with my version of a courtroom amen — "Remember Buster."

Bill understood. Now that he had won the first of what we hoped would be many races, he too would have to develop his own way of remembering Buster.

IV
Conversations

THE GENTLY ROLLING HILLS AND GREEN VELVET valleys, normally dotted with picnicking families or young lovers, became a nightmare of agony for the "thin clads." Every rise in elevation, no matter how slight, strained their energy and challenged their stamina as they numbly battled each other and fatigue to finish the race.

As I watched the weary runners mechanically pump their leadened legs, I wondered what force was driving each of them on. Was Bill, because of the numbness which pain and suffering mercifully bring, now motivated subconsciously by the highest and most inspirational thoughts? Surely some of the others were running for status, prestige, glory, and fame. Would this sustain them more than love, faith, and desire? Though we had talked about the obligations that accompany victory, we had never talked about the prestige, status, and wealth that can come with it.

When you sit in a sauna, sweat dripping from every pore, skin glistening, stomach feeling just a little "oozy," you feel a kinship with the rugged, hearty Finnish folk who gave us this tradition. Somehow, to talk about anything besides the basic virtues they lived by seems inappropriate. But maybe we should have talked about these other things more; perhaps that would have helped Bill in his quest for victory and success.

Success. Bill and I talked about the meaning of success only months before this, his biggest race.

"Dad, who is the most successful man you know?" Bill asked as we entered the steamy redwood sauna.

"Before I can answer that," I said, "we have to define *success*. I think a friend of mine once summed it up the best when he said, 'True success is the ability to accept and give love.' If this is the definition of success, Bill — and I believe it is — then the most successful man I have ever known is Ralph Shepard."

I first met Ralph Shepard some ten years earlier when the retired superintendent of schools entered my office and asked if he could in any way assist our volunteer program.

Will Rogers once said that anyone over forty is responsible for how he looks. Well, I looked at this gray-haired, smiling man standing before me and I instantly saw the very personification of love. His whole face, his whole being, seemed to express love.

After we talked awhile about the volunteer program, I said, "Ralph, we are going to call you a 'presentence investigator.' But please don't let that confuse you. We just want you to love people."

From that day until the day he died some years later, Ralph loved the defendants who appeared before our court. What Ralph did for them was incredible. In a typical case a young defendant, often in his late teens, would plead or be found guilty. I would declare, "Guilt having been determined, the court will refer you to the presentence department for an investigation. Sentencing will be adjourned for three weeks until we get their report and study it."

The defendant — hatred, fear, frustration, and anger welling up inside — would resist the urge to hit me only because he knew he would get into worse trouble. Then he would stalk out of the courtroom. Day after day I stared into hate-filled eyes. But when the defendant entered Ralph's office, Ralph did not, or perhaps could not, see the hatred. He saw only hurt in those eyes.

"During the first twenty minutes of our presentence investigation, the defendant screams, shouts, swears, and snarls at me," Ralph told me. "But I like to smoke a pipe during these interviews, and now that I'm old I have to fumble for the pouch and can never find it very fast. When I do find it, it takes me a long time to pack it right. I never get it the way I want it the first time, so I have to unload and repack. I usually have to repeat this whole operation two or three times before I get it right. Now obviously, during this time, I can't yell back and defend myself or the court. Packing my pipe requires too much concentration. I can only listen.

"Finally, after twenty minutes I take my first triumphant puff on the pipe, lean back, and say, 'Son, let's chat.'"

Now how can you stay mad at a person whom you have screamed at for twenty minutes when all he says in reply is, "Son, let's chat," in a way that really means "I'm interested in you — tell me where and how it hurts."

And chat they did. No professional could have afforded the time. Most presentence interviews, in the very few "lower" courts which conduct them at all, take fifteen minutes or less in a typical misdemeanor case. But in many cases Ralph met the defendant shortly after 8 a.m. At noon they would finally emerge from Ralph's office and head over to the restaurant across the street for a sandwich. Sometimes they even returned to Ralph's office after lunch.

This happened time after time. Many defendants — so angry, so hostile when they walked out of the courtroom — would, after talking with Ralph, return and take a seat in the back of the room. They usually would sit patiently, sometimes for two hours, waiting for a recess. Then they would seek me out and say, "Judge, I have a question. Can Mr. Shepard be my probation officer?"

Ralph did what no one ever did for them before. He enhanced the defendants' dignity by listening. Ralph knew well the secret: If you really want to make someone feel important, worthwhile, and good, listen to him. As Ralph himself said, "Enemies talk, friends listen." To me he personified the title of a book by John W. Drakeford, *The Awesome Power of the Listening Ear.*

"Keith, the trouble with you judges is that you listen only to the words when people talk to you," Ralph once chided me. "Don't listen to the words. They will only confuse you. When people talk to you, listen to the music."

How Ralph would listen to the music! When a defendant snarled at him and said, "I hate you, you old man," Ralph heard, "I'm alone. Please help me."

At the end of a presentence investigation of four hours or more, Ralph would ask the young man or young woman to bring in mother or dad or someone else to speak on his behalf. This request would have been quickly and firmly rejected at the start of a conversation; but as the defendant came to regard Ralph as a friend, he nearly always agreed.

When Ralph did meet the parent or another adult who came to talk for the offender, he verbally disarmed that person also. His first question was, "Tell me about the good things your son does." How can you resist someone who wants to know the good about a person who, in your own way, you love?

Ralph really did want to know the good. He told me, "You have all the people around here you need to tell you the bad. You get the police record and look at it before sentencing. You hear the police officer or the complaining witness describe what happened in the case. You can get FBI reports. You don't need any help getting the bad news. So I'll give you the good news. And don't you ignore it. The bad you must know, because the bad has to be overcome. But the good is also important. It is the good that we can build on, that we *must* build on."

Thus it came to be that I would read in the presentence reports things like, "This boy lives next door to an elderly widow. For years he has been mowing her lawn and won't take any money for it." Or, "This girl lives across the street from a young divorcee with three children. She has been baby-sitting all year while the mother goes to school one night a week and won't take any money for it. She says she has to study anyway and might as well study on one side of the street as the other."

How Ralph's eyes would twinkle with delight and love a few days later in the courtroom when we sentenced "his" defendant. "Mr. Shepard tells us you have been mowing the lawn of that widow for many years," I would say in the solemnity and austerity of my position. "He tells us a lot of other fine things about you. We think you are a fine young man who should never have been involved in this kind of conduct. We also think you are the kind of young man who is not going to get into more trouble. We are expecting you to do really fine things with your life and are looking forward to our year together. We are also looking forward to the end of the year, when we are going to dismiss this case after you have proven to our probation department that Mr. Shepard is right."

Ralph liked that. He always said, "You know, Judge, people will nearly always give you what you expect from them. You expect hate and you will get it. You expect failure and you will get it. Above all, if you expect accomplishment and achievement, you will usually get it."

But technically speaking, Ralph was the worst presentence investigator in history. He could, and often would, spend three or four hours with a young man or woman and not even find out a home address. He would learn almost nothing about them factually. He would know little about their school or work record. He really knew nothing — and everything — about the defendant. He could, and did, paint a most beautiful word-picture of the emotional turmoil in the life of offenders. He was not only a musician, he was also an artist.

Of course, we had to know many more things about the defendant. To do this we utilized the volunteer services of Lou Loeffert, a retiree who had investigated labor disputes for the railroad for forty-eight years. He was an uncanny investigator. We used to say that Lou could find out more about you in fifteen minutes than you knew. He would gather the facts — the work record, the school record, the criminal record, the family records, and all the other facts so important to a good investigation. His thoroughness and the crispness of his mind were a never-ending source of amazement for us, and we depended on Lou Loeffert.

The third member of our presentence investigation team was Bill H., also a retiree. Bill was, we would say, an alcoholic. Bill would say he *is* an alcoholic. He had a great amount of trouble with drinking and finally, after many years, received the hospitalization and professional help he so desperately needed, then joined Alcoholics Anonymous. Each defendant who appeared before us on a drinking-related offense met Bill, who would determine whether the offender was an experimenter, an occasional drinker who got a little carried away, or an alcoholic.

Assisting the three were volunteer psychiatrists, psychologists, medical doctors, attorneys, and other professionals. They did four things vital to such investigations: helped the judge to determine sentence; diverted medical and other cases from the criminal justice system that should never have come there in the first place; developed a probational plan of rehabilitation; and constantly demanded that we expand our services until we had every rehabilitative technique needed to carry out their suggestions.

But Ralph Shepard added a fifth dimension. He prepared the offender for an experience with a probation department that really cared and loved in a demanding, firm, disciplined manner. How well he did this job! Because of Ralph and the others, I will always believe we had the finest presentence department in the country.

Only one other time did I come into contact with someone who completely changed the entire atmosphere of a courtroom and probation department the way Ralph did. I entered an unfamiliar building in a western city one morning, and a voice rang out, "Can I help you, sir?" I had never before been greeted that way in a probation department, and this took me by surprise. I saw a young man in a wheelchair sitting under a sign that said, INFORMATION.

As I stood disconcerted, the young man continued, "It sure is a nice day, isn't it? Are you a stranger to our city?"

I nodded, and he asked, "Who do you want to see?" When I replied, he gave me directions and I turned to leave. His words wafted back, "Have a good day!"

Incredible! It was so unlike the usual impersonal atmosphere of a probation department, I couldn't get over it.

A few minutes later I was in the office of the chief probation officer on my mission of helping them to start using volunteers. I mentioned the young man downstairs. The chief probation officer told me the man had been a fine high school athlete, but shortly before graduation was injured in an automobile accident. As a result, he would be confined to a wheelchair for the rest of his life. The officer said, "Do me a favor. As you talk to people today, ask them who the most important employee in this building is. I would appreciate it."

I talked to about fifteen members of the probation department's staff that day, and at the end of each conversation I asked, "Who is the most important employee in this building?" Everyone said, without hesitation, "That's easy — the boy in the wheelchair. Before he came here, nearly every parent came in angry and ready to fight. I used to hate coming to work. But now a completely different attitude and atmosphere flows through these halls. Working is fun again. Now, when the parents and others come in all mad and upset, the young man greets them and they talk for a few minutes. As they leave, he says something like, 'I'm glad that you have Probation Officer Brown. You'll really like him. He really loves kids. Not only does he work here about fifty hours a week, but he spends about ten hours a week coaching Little League teams.'"

Every probation officer I met that day said the young man had created a whole new attitude and atmosphere. He was a volunteer who came down to the court each day in his wheelchair and gave freely of his time. I thought of Ralph.

Bill knew Ralph too, and I think Bill agreed that success is truly the ability to give and accept love. In that way I consider Ralph the most successful man I have known. He taught me that love is "where it's at." I hoped I was able to pass this on to Bill. What greater gift could a father give a son?

Ralph Shepard also embodied another saying I kept under the wide glass desktop in my courtroom. Kipling said it first: "Be slow to judge. We know little of what has been done and nothing about what has been resisted." Ralph seemed to keep in mind the old Indian adage, "Do not judge a man until you have walked a mile in his moccasins."

Though not a judge, Ralph possessed the single greatest quality needed to be a great judge or a great anything else. He was a decent human being.

This was important to me. I have become concerned by the emphasis of graduate schools — especially law schools — on being "smart." The dean of a large and prestigious law school told me on one of my trips, "We are very proud of our law school. Over 50 percent of our current seniors could not get in if they were applying as freshmen this year."

I should not have said it, but I did: "Oh, that's really a shame. Almost without exception, the best students I have known have done very little for other people. They have gone on to make a lot of money, some of them. But of course, there is no value in that. Nearly all the students I know of who have gone on to really help people and serve their fellowmen have been the 'C' and 'B' students."

The dean became angry, "Statistics do not bear that out at all," he said. I admitted that I had never made a study of it and my remarks were based on personal observation. Fortunately for our host, the conversation was interrupted by a call to sit down to dinner; I am glad I did not have to finish the discussion. I am not sure that I approve of a system which would not tolerate my going to law school because of an average or relatively lower I.Q. I fear that in our quest for brilliance we can lose the importance of the quality of being a decent human being.

In the sauna Bill and I sometimes talked about what it is like to be a judge and about some of the problems a person faces when wearing the judicial robes. It's not difficult to decide guilt or innocence in most cases; that is usually relatively easy. But sentencing a man, deciding how he will spend his immediate future and affecting how he will spend the rest of his life, is tough. I shared with Bill the toughest case I ever faced.

I had been on the bench for only a few weeks when two young men, aged seventeen and nineteen, were brought before me. They pleaded not guilty, and a jury trial was slated.

Testimony revealed that the younger brother, "George," was driving down a street and saw a uniformed police officer. Suddenly, for no reason whatsoever except to impress his passenger, George screamed at the officer, calling him the most profane and obscene names imaginable. He then screeched his tires and sped away. But George did not see the officer's police car parked, with motor running, in the driveway. As the officer jumped into his squad car and sped away in pursuit, he didn't notice that another car also joined the chase.

Quickly overtaking George's car and forcing it into a parking lot, the officer pulled George out the door. George resisted the officer, and as they struggled, the car that had followed the chase screeched to a halt and the driver jumped out.

"I'm his brother! I'm his brother! Be careful, he has a heart condition," the young man shouted as he ran toward the struggling pair.

But the officer either didn't hear or ignored George's brother, "Mark," and continued to push George, who still struggled in vain. Mark shouted his warning a second time; still the officer pushed George. Finally Mark stepped between the two and shoved them apart.

At that moment more officers, alerted by the police radio, arrived at the scene. George and Mark were arrested, George charged with being a disorderly person and Mark with interfering with an officer in the performance of his duties.

The jury listened carefully to the evidence and returned to the courtroom after deliberating for about two hours. It seemed obvious to me that George was guilty, and such was the jury's verdict — guilty as charged.

But what about Mark? I hoped the jury would find him not guilty. A judge is not to convey such hopes to the jury in any way, but he has feelings and opinions even as everyone else does.

"In the second case," the foreman intoned, "we also find the defendant guilty." I felt a sinking feeling in my stomach and a heavy burden on my heart.

I adjourned both cases for final determination and sentencing. I had to make a decision. I could render judgment in accordance with the guilty verdict of the jury, or I could find Mark not guilty in spite of it.

While spending a long Labor Day weekend at beautiful Lake Vermillion in northern Minnesota, I pondered the two cases. The walleyes were biting, the sun was shining, and I was eight hundred miles from home. Yet I couldn't take my mind off those cases. So much seemed to be at stake.

George was clearly guilty — no doubt about that. It was just a matter of sentencing. Since it was his first offense as an adult, and since we didn't have a volunteer program yet, a fine would be appropriate, I decided.

But Mark? That was a problem. Deep in my heart I knew the jury was wrong and the case against Mark should be dismissed.

But the consequences of such a decision overwhelmed me. The police officer in the case talked every chance he had about the court going "soft" on criminals. If I overruled the jury and set Mark free, the policeman would be outraged and complain to his fellow officers that there was no sense in even taking a case to court. And he would have listening ears, for nearly everyone judges a new jurist by what he does in his first few months on the bench. He is quickly labeled as tough or soft, a "police judge" or a "defendant's judge," and it is hard to cast off that label, whether or not it is true.

If I, as a new judge, were to set aside a jury verdict of guilty and find the defendant not guilty, most assuredly I would be labeled a soft judge who hated the police and would do anything for defendants.

I talked to the veteran clerk to ascertain whether any of my predecessors had ever set aside a jury's verdict. She did not know a judge could do such a thing and in her ten years as clerk had never seen it done.

What to do? Should I ignore the right, as God gave me the power to see the right, and do the "greater good" so that this officer and other officers would not "bad-mouth" the court? In times like this I fervently wished I could be considered separate from the court. If it were only hatred, contempt, and disrespect for me as an individual, the decision would be easy. But I *was* the court, and disrespect and hatred for me equaled disrespect and hatred for the court.

What was the greater good — maintain the image of the court in the eyes of the police so they would continue to bring to court the appropriate cases? Or dismiss this case knowing full well that some — a minority, but some — policemen would use this as an excuse not to do their jobs? They would simply not bring proper cases to court.

I could, of course, do only one thing. During my first day on the bench after our return from Minnesota, I said to the defendants, the officers, and everyone else in court: "The defendant, 'George Smith,' is found guilty and is sentenced to pay a fine of $50. In the second case the defendant, 'Mark Smith', is found not guilty."

It was a disaster! The mother of the defendants was furious, believing both her boys should be found not guilty. The brothers stalked out of the courtroom and returned to their homes angry at the "stupid judge" who had found George guilty and made him pay a fine. The officer stamped from the courtroom and did not bring another case to court for some time.

I often wondered — after we had developed complete rehabilitative services, using volunteers and professionals — how many cases that officer and others he influenced just ignored and let go, how many involving offenders we really could have helped.

Some friends who had supported me when I ran for judge told me they had heard I "let kids go" even after a jury found them guilty. It was fortunate that they came to me so I could explain what had happened. But I worried about the hundreds of others who had heard the story and did not think enough of us to ask to hear our side.

"Bill," I began one night in the sauna after we had discussed the rough start I had as a judge, "sometimes the wrong seems so much easier. It would be so convenient to take the easy way out. It would please so many people. But for some reason, I do not know why, it just doesn't work out right that way. You have to do the right as God gives you the power to see the right. There simply isn't any other way. Nothing else works."

Bill seemed to understand these conversations, and I think he really took them to heart.

Unfortunately I did not always do the right thing, and I shared some of these severely painful memories with Bill also. The worst experience of all was a case in which two human lives were lost.

"Jack," a strong eighteen-year-old, was called "the Enforcer" by his gang and took it upon himself to avenge the "wrongs" suffered by his buddies. One day he walked into a drive-in restaurant and for no apparent reason started to hit the guard, who was sitting in a booth. Jack struck him repeatedly and left him beaten and dazed.

Jack was arrested and brought before me. He pleaded not guilty, but a jury returned a guilty verdict. We ran a twenty-hour presentence investigation after the trial, and all the facts about his role as the "hatchet man" of the gang surfaced, along with the history of a sad childhood.

It was a difficult case to sentence. There was little organized gang activity in our city, and we all hoped to keep it that way. And Jack's needs were great.

We fined Jack and ordered him to make restitution for the damages he had caused. In this case it meant paying the guard's doctor and hospital bills, plus paying for the damage done to the restaurant. We also decided to sentence him to thirty days in jail. At my request he was kept in the city lockup, where he had an individual cell, rather than in the county jail, where he would have been in a "bull pen" with other prisoners.

The presentence reports included a report from a volunteer psychologist and a volunteer psychiatrist and our own official staff. I became convinced we had to do two things: First, convince this defendant that there is a right and a wrong, and wrongdoing means punishment. Once that fact had been established by jailing him, there was a second need — help the defendant see that there is a better way and see how to live his life in that better way. To accomplish this, we assigned Jack to a group psychotherapy session where he met with one of our volunteer psychiatrists and about eight to twelve other young offenders who were among the most hostile and difficult probationers in our court.

Jail time in the individual cell for Jack was hard. In my decade as judge, on many occasions we actually had men request thirty days in the county jail rather than five days in an individualized city jail cell. Eventually we came to equate one day in the city jail to five days in the county.

After about seven days two police officers whom I respected (I had deep respect for most of the officers in our city) requested of me that Jack be allowed to leave his cell and wash police cars during the daytime. I believed he should not be given this privilege, so I refused. Three days later they returned and requested the same privilege. I told them that if they still felt that way after three more days, I would agree. They came again three days later and, as promised, I granted their request.

On two or three occasions after that they and other officers requested a shortening of the jail term. I refused until two days before Jack was scheduled to leave. At that time he was brought before me and I carefully explained the terms of probation to him. Since he was a heavy drinker, he was required to attend the Alcohol and Drug Addiction School run by an excellent teacher, a recovered alcoholic. He was also assigned to a one-to-one volunteer after three months of group psychotherapy. He was well programmed with meetings, reporting to someone about four hours a week during the first two months, including his weekly meetings with the regular staff.

One of the rules governing our group psychotherapy sessions required the psychiatrist to tell members of the probation staff, including me, only two facts about the group's members — whether the defendant was or was not showing up for the meetings, and whether any progress was being made. This and nothing more.

When I talked to the psychiatrist after their fourth meeting, he told me Jack was reporting and making progress. Off the record he added a rare third statement.

"If Jack does not get himself into an extremely aggravating situation in the next two months or so," the psychiatrist said, "he will make it. He is really progressing." It appeared as though our procedure of being tough for the first month was working.

But a few days later Jack was at a drive-in restaurant and, according to him, was taunted by another boy. The teasing went beyond Jack's point of toleration and he left, got a gun, returned, and killed the boy.

Jack appeared again in our court, this time on a very serious charge — murder. We conducted a preliminary hearing only in felony cases and, finding that a crime had been committed and that there was probable cause for thinking Jack did commit the crime, we sent the case on to the higher court for trial.

Jack was convicted of murder and sent to prison. About a year later we received word that he himself had been killed in a prison fight.

This will always be the ultimate example of failure for me as a judge. We lost not one life, but two. How badly can you fail?

I have relived that case a thousand times. Why didn't I send a volunteer into the jail every day for those thirty days? We often had volunteers go to jail so that the relationship could begin immediately, rather than after the jail term. Why not in this case? Or why didn't we allow him to come over once a week for group meetings during those thirty days? Was it really necessary to be so tough for so long? Why didn't I listen to the officers sooner? A thousand why's.

We did what we honestly thought was best, but it did not work out that way. It is easy, of course, to tell the other guy not to second-guess and look back, but you can't tell yourself that. It is easy to excuse others, but it is hard to excuse yourself, particularly when your failure involves the loss of human life.

Perhaps the most reassuring thing you can tell yourself at such a time is that we are responsible for obedience, not results. I believe this to be true. If I did not believe it, the burden of such cases would be unbearable. Obedience to God and to self requires that we handle each case with meticulous care and do the very best we possibly can. We are responsible for obedience. If we were responsible for results on every occasion we would soon be driven to suicide.

I tried to make this philosophy part of Bill's life. I hoped he would handle this, his big race, in that way.

"Bill, when you run," I sought to teach him, "remember always that you are responsible for obedience — to do your best and to finish as well as you can. But never forget that you are not responsible for results. We obey and God resolves. You do not have the responsibility to finish first or for any other result."

The odds were overwhelmingly against his finishing high enough to make All-State. I knew he had performed well in his responsbility for obedience. He had trained well and very hard. One time in the sauna he let me get a glimpse beyond this race. Bill said he wanted at least to try to run in college, and at a college where he would run with and against the best. And then he hesitantly expressed the ultimate hope — harbored tentatively and secretly by all those who ran in the state finals: "The Olympics."

If Bill didn't achieve all his goals, I only hoped he could remember my great failure with Jack and not be crushed by failure to attain what he so fervently sought.

Above: *Bill runs in a league meet as his mother (right, in dark coat) cheers him on.*

Right: *Judge Leenhouts gives one of his frequent addresses about volunteer programs.*

V
The Fatherless

$\mathbf{W}$HO IS TO BE PITIED MORE THAN THE FATHERLESS? How often in the Scriptures we see the fatherless singled out as "the least of all of these," those to whom we owe the greatest duty of all. Time and again the point is made with great force and clarity. The greatest duty is owed to the very least, the most luckless, the downtrodden, the oppressed, those hurting the most, those who continually suffer — those whom the Bible often characterizes by one word: — *fatherless.*

"Defend the fatherless," demands Isaiah 1:17. "He executes justice for the fatherless," reads Deuteronomy 10:18.

I have often wondered if our nation — if we, above all — should be the most pitied as a nation of fatherless people. How often I saw evidence of this in court.

The defendant of one of my earliest cases, a father about twenty-eight-years old, appeared in our court charged with beating his wife. When his wife appeared in my office to give the brief description under oath necessary for a complaint and warrant to be issued, she added softly and tearfully, "When he is sober he is wonderful. But when he drinks . . ."

A few hours later at the arraignment the defendant pleaded guilty and asked to be sentenced immediately. "I'm guilty, just go ahead and sentence me," he said.

But I told him that more information was needed before sentencing. I asked his wife to testify under oath. I think the defendant was not too pleased, but we took her testimony anyway, and I soon realized why he wanted to leave the courtroom as quickly as possible.

"Last night," the wife began, tears welling in her eyes and voice shaking, "he came home drunk again. He really is a wonderful man except when he gets drunk. When I heard him come in the door I knew he was drunk, because he always slams the door when he's drunk. Then I heard him walking around downstairs, bumping against the walls, and I knew he was pretty drunk. I was scared, for he often beats me when he comes home like this.

"But this time it was different. If it had only been me he beat and humiliated, I wouldn't have come to court. This time he stumbled up the stairs and began waking up our four young children. The oldest is only eight, and the youngest is three. He screamed and swore at them as he told them to get right downstairs to the living room.

"The children ran crying and screaming down the stairs as he came in to get me. 'You rotten — !' he swore. 'You think that I don't know what is going on around here. You think I'm so stupid I don't know. But I do.' He grabbed me and pulled me out of bed, ripping my nightgown until I was almost naked. He grabbed me by the hair and arms and began to push, shove, and pull me down the stairs. When we got into the living room, I was barely conscious of the presence of the children huddled in one corner of the room.

"Then he screamed at the kids, 'Now watch this, you little brats! I'm going to show you who is boss! Make no mistake about it and don't forget this!' He started to hit me with his fist. He hit me in the eye, the one that is all bruised and closed today. I fell down, but he yanked me off the floor and hit me again, in the stomach. I fell again, and again he pulled me off the floor and hit me. I don't know how many times this went on, but he finally stopped and told the kids once again that they had better never forget who was the boss of this house. Then he staggered up to bed and fell asleep across the bed with his clothes on.

"The children and I waited until eight o'clock before we went to the police station. I wouldn't have gone to the police if it had only been me. I never have gone to the police before when he beat me. But this time it wasn't just me. Why did he have to wake up the children?"

The defendant was crying. The children, sitting in the front row, were crying too.

America, with all her wealth, power, and prestige. Are we the most fatherless nation of all? Are our people to be pitied more than any others on earth? Psalm 10:14 says, ". . . helper of the fatherless." Again in verse 18, ". . . to do justice to the fatherless."

"Mike" and I first met in 1962. He looked like many other seventeen-year-olds except for a distorted left eye. His right eye focused normally, but his left rolled grotesquely and uncontrollably to one side. As a result, he looked like a cliche portrait of a thief who could not look you straight in the eye. Though he could not help his appearance, he lived up to that portrait. He had a long record of shoplifting offenses both as a juvenile and as an adult. (In Michigan the law considers you an adult at seventeen.)

When Mike appeared before our court charged with theft, we placed him on probation and assigned him to a volunteer. Difficult, strained months passed before the volunteer was able to establish a good relationship with Mike. When he finally did, Mike told him, "People don't trust me. I look like a crook with my bad eye. I don't seem to be able to hold onto a job. When I can't find work, I still want things, and the only way I can get them is to steal."

The volunteer referred Mike to one of the several optometrists who volunteered their time to our program. He checked out Mike's wandering eye and discovered it was completely worthless — Mike was blind in that eye.

The optometrist had a friend who was an eye surgeon. He told the surgeon about Mike and about the thousands of hours volunteered to our court by all kinds of people. The surgeon agreed to remove the eye and give Mike a false eye that would not distort his appearance, and do it all as a volunteer without fee.

The mother readily agreed, and Mike was very happy with the idea. But a few days later his mother sadly told us Mike's father disapproved of the operation. When she and Mike had gone home to tell the father the good news, he was drunk. When they asked him about the surgery, the father became angry and shouted at them, "No doctor is going to touch his eye! He was born that way, and that's the way he is going to stay! And besides that, no doctor ever does anything for nothing. He'll send us a big bill and then sue us. He won't go to the doctor as long as I'm here!"

Again it was a case of someone with a father being fatherless. The story had a happy ending only because Mike's father left the home a few months later and disappeared. Mike then had the operation, and we became very proud of him and the fact that he became a law-abiding citizen.

Are we, as Americans, really the poorest nation of all? Are we failing to meet the extremely vital and critical need for fatherhood? Are we among the most pitied of all? The fatherless.

We read more in the Scriptures about the fatherless. God is described as "Father of the fatherless" in Psalm 68:5. In Psalm 146:9 we read, "The Lord . . . upholds . . . the fatherless."

"Harry" came into court in 1965. He had been living with four other seventeen-year-old kids, all of whom had dropped out of school, left home, and shared an apartment. Reading over the names, I immediately recognized Harry's — the same as one of Detroit's most distinguished attorneys. The youth's name bore a "Junior."

We decided to do a presentence investigation. In due course we discovered Harry was indeed the son of the attorney, whom I knew mostly by reputation. He was the recognized authority in his field in Michigan and probably earned more than $100,000 a year.

We notified the parents, as was our custom, and requested that they come in and see us. Harry's mother responded, and we talked with her. Her story was sad but all too familiar to us. She said her husband would have absolutely nothing to do with Harry since it became apparent in about the fourth grade that Harry was not going to be an outstanding student, a "super-noodle," as his father put it. After that, all the father's attention turned to Harry's older brother and younger sister, who were "super-noodles."

The father bragged to his friends about the other children in Harry's presence, but he never bragged about Harry. Harry began to withdraw and seemed to have less and less to offer other people.

Then he found some other youngsters he could talk to and who would listen to him. They were all outcasts, even though they came from one of Detroit's most fashionable suburbs. When Harry started to get into trouble with the juvenile court, his father refused to see Harry except when ordered to by the court.

We asked whether Harry's father would come to court if we wrote and invited him to meet with our presentencing staff. The mother said she doubted it very much, but we decided to try. But Harry's father did not show up or respond in any way.

I decided to call him. When I identified myself on the phone and asked him whether he had received our request, so we could have a better idea of how to sentence Harry, his answer was, "I'll tell you how to sentence him. Give him all the jail time you can. Give him the full ninety days. And when he comes out and gets into trouble, give him ninety days more. Then when he commits a felony, put him in prison for the rest of his life."

Inside I wept for Harry. I could not feel more sorry for anyone than I did for this lonely, embittered, and deeply hurt teenager. Again and again I thanked God for my father who loved me, cared for me, and gave me one of the greatest gifts anyone can have — a father. I thought of the well-known story about two inner-city kids who were talking about a third boy they knew. One said to the other, "He's the luckiest guy in the world. He was born with a silver spoon in his mouth. He has a dad."

The fatherless. More than the persecuted, more than the poor, more than the ill, more than anyone they are to be pitied. Repeatedly the Scriptures tell us that our greatest duty is to the least of the least. And the very least are the fatherless.

Again we read it, ". . . the fatherless who had none to help him" (Job 29:12). In verse 16 we hear it, "I was a father. . . ."

Another seventeen-year-old, "Matt," came to court charged with being drunk and disorderly. Matt had bad teeth. His mouth was too small, and his crowded teeth protruded at wild angles. One suspected they were badly decayed, because he had foul breath.

We assigned Mike to a volunteer. Several months later, after establishing a good relationship, the volunteer suggested Matt go to a dentist. Matt seemed at least mildly interested, but added, "My mother has often wanted to take me, but my dad says he will beat her — and me — if she wastes his money like that. Sometimes my mother says, 'Let's go anyway, one more beating won't make that much difference.' But somehow we have never been to a dentist."

The volunteer, a social worker, arranged for Matt to go to the dental school of a nearby university. Under the direction of the professor, students in dental school fix the teeth of the poor. Several visits later, Mike's teeth were clean and repaired.

"Now I feel like I can be somebody," Matt said. But the volunteer knew it took more than good teeth, and he suggested to Matt that he finish high school. At first Matt did not want to return to school, but gradually he became interested in evening classes. He finally decided to go — a decision that did not come easily for him.

The volunteer was elated until the next meeting with Matt. Matt opened the conversation by saying, "I told my dad I wanted to go to night school. But he just looked at me, laughed, and said, 'You're too dumb to go to school. You should work a second job. Now, that would pay off. School will never pay off for a stupe like you.'

"I guess he's right — I'm too stupid," Matt said softly.

Again the Bible says: "Give justice to . . . the fatherless"

(Ps. 82:3). James 1:27 tells us, "Religion that is pure . . . is this: to visit orphans [the fatherless]."

Not all cases coming to court involve the fatherless. Let no one get the idea that every time a young person gets into trouble with the law it can be traced to a poor father or mother. When you involve yourself with human behavior, nothing is *never* or *always*. We're too complex for such absolutes.

Before I became a judge I met a twelve-year-old boy we will call "Tom." I watched Tom grow through his early and middle teens. When he was seventeen he first appeared before our court on a minor charge. During our presentence investigation a volunteer psychologist spent several hours with his parents and with Tom. Then he told me this:

"Tom has very fine parents. All of his brothers and sisters have done very well. When Tom was quite young, his parents sensed something was wrong with him and began to spend a lot of time with him. But nothing seemed to help. Tom's dad tried to get him interested in church-league sports. He even coached Tom's team — just for Tom — but it didn't seem to help. They took him to psychologists and psychiatrists at an early age to try to get him help. Tom was so young he thought he was only going to see a friend.

"I think the parents did all they could, with love, affection and intelligence. I can find no fault with them. Neither does Tom. But Tom kept getting into more and more trouble. I'm afraid he is headed toward a felony. You know, Judge," the psychologist summed up for me, "there are three things that cause this kind of behavior. One is heredity, one is environment, and the other is the imponderables. This is a case of the imponderables. Everyone of us, no matter how well we love, is subject to the imponderables."

Tom did commit a felony later and went to prison. But he "bottomed out" and now is volunteering his time to offenders who are in trouble with the law because of drugs and alcohol, two things that were involved when he went to prison. He is doing much good now, and I am extremely proud of him.

What caused Tom to go to prison then and to become so important in the lives of others now? The imponderables.

But mostly, perhaps as much as 85 percent of the time, crime seems to involve the fatherless.

The greatest burden of all has been placed upon fathers. When asked about God, Jesus described Him as being like a father.

Are we going to reverse the vicious and deadly cycle of crime in America? My neighboring city of Detroit is rivaling all others for the dubious distinction of being the "murder capital of the world." Detroit, much smaller and less crowded than Tokyo, had approximately three hundred times more murders in 1972 than Japan's largest city. Our country has the highest crime rate in the world.

Why? Does the answer become clearer? Are we a nation of the fatherless? Is that why we murder and maim? Do we cry out, as did Thomas Wolfe in *Look Homeward Angel* when he could not love and be loved by his father, "Oh lost, and by the wind grieved, ghost come back again"?

VI

People Change People

THE LATE JUDGE PAUL ALEXANDER OF TOLEDO, OHIO, a great juvenile court jurist, displayed a sign in his courtroom for many years that read, "Attitudes are not changed by platitudes. Human conduct is changed by human contact. People change people."

In 1969 in Little Rock, Arkansas, I learned a new appreciation for these words when I met Luther Black. My experience with Luther had a profound influence on my life.

As I spoke to a group of professionals and citizens about the use of volunteers with juvenile offenders, my attention was drawn to a graying black man who sat in the first row. He seemed to just sit there and glow as if there were too much goodness in his soul for such a flimsy barrier as skin to contain it. Love radiated from this man, and I sensed that in spite of the fact he had not said one word all night, he completely dominated the entire room. He was one of the most beautiful human beings I had ever seen, and I was fascinated by him. I had to get to know him.

After my speech I pressed through the crowd and introduced myself. After a few minutes of polite exchanges I said untruthfully, "Mr. Black, I need a ride to the airport tomorrow morning. Could you possibly take me?" After Luther said he would, I further asked if he could join me for breakfast, adding with an even bigger lie, "Luther, I usually like to have a big, leisurely breakfast, so let's meet early."

Generally I gobble a little bread as I run out of the house, late as usual, but I needed to spend some time with this man and discover what made him such a beautiful human being. By this bit of deception I managed to spend almost three hours with Luther Black of Little Rock, Arkansas.

At breakfast the next morning we chatted casually for a little while about the volunteers-in-probation concept. Then I blurted out the question which was really burning in my heart and mind.

"Mr. Black, what makes you who you are?" I knew something magnificent must have occurred. It was like looking at the Grand Canyon: A pioneer did not merely stub his toe, nor did an Indian simply kick the dirt some years ago; rather, incredible forces worked wonders to create one of the world's most glorious valleys. The same had to be true of Luther. He did not glow with love for himself and others without something great having happened.

Luther smiled. "Who I am and what I am? Why, what I am really goes back to when I was eight years old. Though it was about fifty years ago, I remember it like yesterday. I was born the youngest of seventeen children on a sharecropper's farm in Arkansas. When I was eight, my mother and father made two huge sacrifices so that I might go to school. First, they bought me some clothes and shoes, and second, they decided they could get along without my help in the fields. I was the first one in the family ever to go to school.

"I remember that first day in school very well. I had never been separated from my brothers and sisters before, and I was terrified. To cover up my fear, I made noise. I kicked the chair in front of me and talked loudly. I was very frightened, and the more frightened I became, the noisier I got.

"Suddenly a huge figure loomed over me. I slowly raised my head and looked into the stern but kind face of my teacher. She looked down at me and said softly, 'Little Black, come to the front of the room.' She called me Little Black because I was the youngest member of the Black family. I warily followed her, knowing she was going to paddle me and send me home. I just knew she was going to kick me out of school. What a disappointment I would be to my family! My dad would be very angry and spank me something awful when I got home, I just knew."

"'Little Black,' she interrupted my thoughts and fears as she sat down in her big chair, 'Little Black, read to me. Sit on my lap and read to me.'

"Still trembling, I sat on her lap and began to read. And as I read, she gave me a hug. The more I read, the more she hugged me. She was a big woman, and soon I disappeared into her lap and bosom. But suddenly I was not afraid anymore, and I have never really been afraid since.

"A few weeks after that, our class held a spelling bee and somehow I reached the finals. But then they gave me a word I did not know. It was one of those words that has an _i_ and an _e_ in it. I didn't know then, and to this day I still can't remember, which comes first. Is it _i_ before _e_ except after _c_, or _e_ before _i_ except before _c_ — or what? I can't remember.

"Nervously I shuffled my feet, stared at the floor, and was about to sit down in defeat when I heard my teacher clear her throat and cough. As I looked up at her she smiled, winked, and pointed at her eye. I knew the next letter just had to be _i_. So I said the letter _i_, spelled the rest of the word correctly, and won the contest. No one ever knew she had helped me. It was our secret.

"That teacher gave me love when I needed it most. She helped me achieve a victory when I could not earn it by myself. Sometimes I think that's really what love is — helping someone to get a victory and be proud of himself when he cannot do it himself. And do it secretly so everyone else thinks he did it all by himself.

"You know, she was the most important teacher I ever had, yet I don't remember a single word she said other than 'Little Black, sit on my lap and read to me.' Isn't it interesting! — the most important teacher I ever had, and I hardly remember a word she said. I guess what she taught me was important, but not nearly so important as the fact that she really loved me and helped me to get something I could not get by myself — victory, achievement, accomplishment, dignity, pride, self-respect, and self-love.

"I went on to the University of Arkansas and graduated, then did graduate work at Columbia University. I later became the Director of Public Instruction, Adult Division, for the State of Arkansas. I have received awards, honors, and responsibilities. Plaques and certificates line the walls of my home.

"But the most important thing that ever happened to me was when my teacher put me on her lap and hugged me."

Bill and I talked about Luther Black and his great testimonial to the heart and soul of what my life is all about. If you really want to change the attitude and conduct of the defendant who appears before your court, you must wrap up the love and concern you have for him in a person who really cares, who listens, who loves, who shares, who disciplines, and who really gives of himself to the apprehended offender.

Luther Black truly summed up what my life should be all about, both as a judge and as a father. I should try very hard to show, not merely talk about my love for Bill. Talk is cheap and means little. Words do not mean much unless they become flesh and blood. When I told our sons that I loved them, did the words become flesh in my life? Or were they only words? The answer to that would determine if I were really a father or simply the husband of their mother.

*W*OULD MY LOVE FOR BILL, AS LUTHER BLACK HAD put it, *"help someone to achieve a victory — to be proud of himself — when he might not be able to do it all by himself,"* I wondered as I alternately ran and walked along with the other spectators to the three-quarter-mile mark where we would next see the runners flash by. There the lazy, rolling green hills were abruptly interrupted by a dense, century-old forest breached only by a small trail that would guide the runners through the dark, damp maze. Weeks before, while Bill had jogged around the course, the rest of our family had searched for the best vantage points; now I leaned breathlessly against the scarred trunk of a familiar, aging pine where I knew I could watch Bill for two hundred yards.

Gasping for breath out of excitement and exertion, I cursed my poor physical condition as a lone runner burst over the crest of the hill — not Bill. I began another eternity of waiting, looking, and counting as the solitary leader bounded gracefully down the grassy slope and headed toward the sunless depths of the forest. Then a swarm of bodies and a moving entanglement of arms and legs moved over the top of the hill. *Two, three, four, five. Where is our son?* The horrible thoughts raced again through my mind. *Did an unbearable stomach cramp or an agonizing charley horse force him out?*

The throng of skinny, red-faced boys kept coming. *Ten . . . thirteen . . . sixteen . . . nineteen . . . there he is!* My heart sank. He was running in twentieth place and laboring very hard. He wanted that All-State honor badly in spite of the fact that everything indicated he would not make it. He had to finish among the top fifteen of this race to realize his goal and dream. Twentieth place was not good enough.

No, Bill! You've got to make your move now. You can't do it later, I thought. As if he had heard me, Bill suddenly swung to the outside and spurted from twentieth to sixth place in less than one hundred yards.

"Go Ba-ee!" I yelled as he streaked by me. "Ba-ee" — our sentimental, perhaps even silly nickname for Bill had slipped out. When his younger brother, Dave, had first started talking, he could not say "Billy." "Ba-ee" was the closest he could come, and over the years we used "Ba-ee" lovingly to tease Bill. But never had we called him this outside our home.

My elation suddenly turned to fear as he headed for the trees. Did he use up too much energy? He had more than two miles to go. Would he have any strength left? But he was in sixth place. If he could maintain that place and pace, he would fulfill his dream — All-State — and gain the victory.

We had talked about prayer and the power of God in relationship to running, and decided Bill should not ask God for a victory. The other runners wanted victory just as badly as he did. But as in all the challenges we faced in life, we knew we should pray for strength to do our best and, if victory was in God's plan, to use that victory for His glory. If defeat was in God's plan, we should use that defeat for His glory. We paraphrased Job 1:21 and had our own saying: "The Lord gives victory. The Lord gives defeat. Blessed be the name of the Lord."

Suddenly Bill stumbled slightly, and vigorously shook his right leg every time he raised it off the ground. *Oh no, what's wrong?* I thought. My heart pounded in my ears and temples, beads of sweat formed in the furrows of my brow, and tears welled in my burning eyes as I strained to see what had happened to him.

There it was! A wood chip had stuck to the spikes of his right shoe, and Bill was desperately trying to shake it off, risking a charley horse with each kick. In his attempts to dislodge the chip he drastically slowed his pace. The runners he had just passed were swiftly catching up.

At last, after a seeming eternity which lasted about twenty seconds, the villain chip flew high into the air and came to rest beside the path. Bill resumed his normal pace and turned toward the clump of trees. I knew I would not see him again for about five minutes, while he ran the mile through the woods. I could only wait, worry, and wonder.

There was no way I could know how Bill was doing back in those woods. What other sport is there quite like this one? In football, you don't lose sight of the players and the score several times during the game. You surely do in cross-country. Oh, how I hate and love the sport!

When Bill finally emerged at the two-mile mark he could be first, last, or anywhere in between, or he might not come out of those woods at all. He could be limping in with a pulled muscle or bent over vomiting beside the course.

VII
The Positive Influence of Others

WHEN I CAME HOME AT NIGHT WHILE BILL WAS very young, he would immediately drop his toy fire engine, blocks, or other playthings and run for me, jumping up and down and shouting, "Daddy! Daddy! You're home! Yeah! Daddy's home!"

He would put his tiny, dirty hand in mine and take me on an exciting journey through the backyard wilderness where imaginary rustlers, dragons, or monsters lurked behind every shrub. After a meal in his fort, castle, covered wagon, or whatever shelter he wished our house to be, we spent the rest of the evening playing, laughing, and enjoying each other.

His beautiful mother was Bill's world during the day, but when I got home I was his whole world. And though I sometimes wished for a moment of privacy, I really loved every minute.

I realized, watching this race, that not many months hence Bill would leave for college, and our life together as we had known it would end. How quickly our time together would be over! With what amazing speed I would be left with the empty shell of his bedroom and a churning mix of memories.

Yet practically from the beginning I knew that perhaps my most important and difficult task as a father was to prepare

Bill for this departure and a life in which I would no longer be the central figure — in fact, a life in which I would no longer even be necessary. A father can be the sole inspirational personality in the life of his son for only so long. Then the son must see and emulate inspiring qualities in others. What a joyful-sad paradox of parenthood — if Bill could not form positive and meaningful relationships with others, if I did not work hard to become unnecessary, I would be a tragic failure as a parent.

The inescapable and good, but painful and heartbreaking turning point of our life together came when Bill entered junior high school. My wife and I were anxious and concerned that our shy, awkward son, having performed so poorly in grade school and experiencing the confusing change to young manhood, would withdraw unto himself in his new school filled with 800 mostly unfamiliar students. Thus we strongly encouraged Bill to form positive relationships with others by involving himself in some kind of extracurricular activity, be it drama, sports, band, French club, or some other. So, probably to please us more than anything else, Bill decided to try out for football.

After his first day of practice Bill ran into the house and excitedly told us about "Mr. Conley," the new young coach from Iowa and Minnesota.

"Mr. Conley said I ought to be able to make some touchdowns for the school!" Bill exclaimed. I had never seen him so enthusiastic; his big eyes glowed with the expectation of a relationship that was to have a profound effect upon Bill, upon me, and upon some of the probationers in our court. When it came to kids, I was soon to discover, Jim Conley was without a weakness.

Jim's intense and sincere enthusiasm quickly infected the entire school, and more than a hundred boys tried out for his lightweight team. Jim cut no one from the squad and played every boy in every game. And somehow they all played in time.

I sought out and began to know the young coach who inspired so many boys to play far better than their abilities normally allowed them. In time I learned that Jim had led a pretty tough life as a youngster. The father, an alcoholic, abandoned the family when Jim was quite young. Soon after, Jim's mother, unable to care for him by herself, placed him in an orphanage. He never saw either parent again as a youngster.

When he was only thirteen, the police caught Jim in a car he had stolen and taken for a joy ride. But the owner, a Methodist minister, declined to prosecute and instead asked the court if the tough, and very hurt, youngster could live with him. The court agreed. Through the minister's positive influence Jim developed into an outstanding athlete, student, and law-abiding citizen.

Hearing his amazing story, I asked Jim if he would consider working with a group of ten difficult, hard-nosed young offenders placed on probation by our own court. Jim agreed and organized the ten into a group he called his "physical education" class.

Jim worked his new group hard. For two hours each week they played basketball, volleyball, and other exhausting games. Then as the ball lay silently by, they worked "soft" — talking quietly about their personal feelings and the problems that had caused them to lash out at society. As the group's one-year probation period was nearing an end I asked Jim how he was doing.

"Just great, Keith," he smiled, his square chin jutting forward. "These guys and I understand each other. You see, I was one of them when I was young."

Though the young offenders in Jim's physical education group were among the most difficult cases passing through our court, not one — to the best of our knowledge — ever got into further trouble with the law.

Jim often visited us in our home and, while becoming a good friend of the entire family, became an especially good friend of Bill's. He had inspired Bill to play football beyond his real ability, and I believe Bill almost thought Jim Conley was just a little bit above God and that God was a little above the rest of us. A man on that kind of pedestal can do so much to help — or hurt — a young, vulnerable boy. Jim used his influence wisely, and Bill benefited greatly from it.

But Jim Conley symbolized a great paradox in my life. I was proud and pleased that Bill had found inspiring qualities in another man. At the same time, however, I was somewhat sad that I was no longer Bill's entire world. Now I had to share him. The painful but necessary process of becoming unnecessary had begun.

When Bill entered the ninth grade he again changed schools. Though all of us wanted his special relationship with Jim to continue, it seemed it would have to end. But in talking with Jim I found out he was to be married and wanted very much to live in the country. Van, my real estate partner, and I had just bought a farm, so we asked Jim and his bride to live there.

Jim and Bill's relationship thrived on that farm. For three summers Bill built up his strength by working the hayfields with Jim. For three summers Bill built up his character by living and talking with Jim Conley.

We eventually had to quit farming because, like so many small farmers in the area, we couldn't survive economically. Jim left the farm when Bill was a junior in high school, and we later sold it. But it had served its purpose well. Jim and Bill became lifelong friends, and Bill would feel Jim's influence athletically, academically, and in other ways throughout his life. Buying that farm was an investment not in real estate, but in Bill.

Jim Conley, as I told Bill, reminded me of St. Paul and that mysterious weakness which forced the apostle to rely, not on his own power, but on God's. Had Paul not had this weakness, he would have relied on himself and become simply a man called Saul who sewed tents in a city called Tarsus. But because of this weakness, Paul had no choice. He had to depend upon the power of another; he chose God.

Relying on God's power, the tentmaker was transformed into an apostle. Paul said, "On my own behalf I will not boast, except of my weaknesses . . . . when I am weak, then am I strong" (2 Cor. 12:5, 10).

Jim Conley's early life and his fine accomplishments with kids later became another example of great strength growing out of weakness.

In time of defeat, Bill and I learned to say, "When I lose, then I win." And thus it was to be.

Bill's heart and mind were also deeply pierced by some of the truly great, inspiring people in this country who visited me professionally and often stayed in our home.

Richard "the Lion-Hearted" Simmons of Seattle, Washington, for example. A wisp of a physical man whose large, dark, penetrating eyes flash through thick, black-framed glasses, Dick is probably the most Christ-centered man I have known. He walks closer to God than any other person I have known. To be with this young minister is to be with Isaiah and the ancient prophets. My private name for Dick is "Ike," short for Isaiah.

In 1965, while deep in prayer, Dick felt called to try to restore the forgotten, lost life of a man in prison. Dick asked the warden of the maximum security state prison, some miles away, for the name of the prisoner who had been there the longest and had had the least contact, by mail or visitors, with the outside world.

Dick began to visit "John," a bitter twenty-five-year-old who had served eight years of a very long sentence for armed robbery. John's mother died when he was eight. Throughout John's trouble-filled childhood his alcoholic father rejected him and severely beat him. During his eight years in prison John received absolutely no visitors, no letters, and no birthday or Christmas cards.

At first John was surly and distrustful during their weekly two-to-three-hour visits. But Dick expected this. One, two, three, then four months passed, and the hostile young man still would not accept Dick's love and friendship. Finally, in utter frustration, Dick wept. Why couldn't he convince the stooped figure with whom he shared the depressing, gray six-by-nine-foot concrete and steel cage that he was there out of love — not to study a psychological freak and write a book? Why couldn't he help this damaged fellowman?

Suddenly Dick lifted his face from his wet hands, for his weeping was not the only sound that broke the gloomy stillness. _Two_ people in the cell were crying. "The Holy Spirit shook the hell in our hearts right out of our bodies," Dick told me later.

From that time on, John became increasingly friendly, talked freely, and looked forward to seeing Dick each week. When

John was paroled, Dick met him at the gate, took him to his home for a meal, saw that he had a place to stay, and later helped him get a job. They kept in close touch, and John finally adjusted to a steady job and a law-abiding life.

Dick's relationship with John has grown into a program called, in various states, either "Job Therapy, Inc." or "Man-to-Man." Through this, Dick and his associates have introduced more than seven thousand citizen-volunteers into the lives of thousands of hopeless, lonely, rejected prisoners. Beginning in prison, through the parole period, and usually beyond, these dedicated, concerned citizen-volunteers do on a one-to-one basis what one friend does for another. They listen. They counsel on family problems and hopes, if any, for the future. They listen. They help in times of crisis. They listen. They assist with particular needs. They listen. They refer to volunteer professionals who assess employment aptitudes and attitudes. They listen. They help find jobs. And they listen.

"How desperate we are to have someone listen to us," a psychologist friend told me. "We used to listen to each other. We sat on big open porches, in comfortable, quiet living rooms, in wicker and straw lawn chairs under big oak trees, and *listened*, really listened, to each other.

"But now it seems as though we don't take the time to talk and listen to each other. The truth is, most of us psychologists would be out of work if people would start listening to each other again. It's sad, really, that people pay me fifty dollars an hour just to listen to them. How desperate we are to have someone listen to us!"

Dick and his volunteers listen. And what does this accomplish? Laymen and professionals working together as volunteers have greatly reduced the rate of return to prison of thousands of hard-core offenders — the "worst of the very worst." The savings in taxpayers' dollars comes to millions. The savings in human values and lives is beyond reckoning.

Dick Simmons and his volunteers inspired Gov. Daniel J. Evans of their state of Washington to say in his keynote address to the 1968 Republican convention: "The greatness of America is not measured by wealth. . . . It is measured by the number of those who visit in the prisons . . . ."

Bill and I listened to those words on the radio while vacationing in northern Minnesota. We knew that the man who had inspired those words had visited our home, had sat with us in our sauna, had slept in the bed next to Bill's. He was Bill's friend and mine. We shared a treasure — Dick "Ike" Simmons.*

Our friend Bob Moffitt, on the other hand, the slim former Peace Corps member with a perpetual smile, has introduced thousands of concerned citizen volunteers into the lives of Denver, Colorado's _juvenile_ offenders through his program called "Partners."

When a Denver probation officer places a juvenile offender on probation, he also asks him if he would like to join the adult-youth organization, Partners. The young offender, hostile to anyone in a position of authority, usually says, "No! I don't want to join any club that you have anything to do with."

"Oh, I'm sorry to hear that," says the probation officer as he slowly and deliberately shuffles the Partner's application form and puts it into his desk drawer. "I guess we'll just have to cancel that airplane ride and fishing trip we had set up for you."

"Wait a minute! What's with the big iron bird and the fish?" The juvenile suddenly gets interested.

"Well, that's part of the club," the probation officer explains, "but if you're not interested — "

"Wait a minute! Maybe I am," the youngster says a bit anxiously.

The probation officer then explains that obligations and responsibilities go along with the fun. "You have to try to become a good citizen, try to commit no more crimes, and meet three hours a week with a citizen of the Denver area whom we will select."

All his life the young juvenile has "conned" his way out of responsibilities and obligations, so he figures he can handle all that other "un-fun-stuff" when it comes along. He'll join just for the initiation day, he thinks — the airplane ride and the fishing — and then he'll quit.

*See "They Go to Prison on Purpose," _Reader's Digest_, August 1970.

A few days later a "Senior Partner" — a volunteer who most likely is in his or her thirties, forties, or fifties — meets the new Junior Partner and they ride with a Partners staff member to the airport. One of several private pilots who volunteer their time, talent, experience, planes, gas, and oil to the program, then seats the youngster in the cockpit, takes off, and circles the greater Denver area for about thirty minutes. Often the pilot lets the boy or girl manipulate the controls for a few seconds. They actually fly the plane. The juvenile offender then comes back down to earth — physically, if not emotionally — where he next visits a nearby trout hatchery. There his hook, bare or baited, attracts thousands of fish. What a day of accomplishment for these otherwise nonachievers: They fly a plane and catch fish.

A few days later the Senior Partner sends to the probationer several pictures, a photo record of their first day together. For the next year of his probation the two Partners attend football games, roller-skate together, ski, and more importantly, talk and listen to each other.

Several times a year a group of as many as a hundred or more Senior and Junior Partners get together for activities such as rafting down the Green River, skiing, tobogganing, and mountain-climbing. At the end of this twelve-month period the young offenders are released from probation and their cases usually dismissed.

Not only are most of these youngsters turned away from a life of crime, but they become inspired and useful citizens who have made, and will continue to make, productive and positive contributions to our society.

With the steam of our sauna surrounding his red face and sweat rolling from his open pores, Bob Moffitt told Bill and me about a frustrated Partners volunteer who once called him with a problem. "The school called and said my kid was cheating," the volunteer had said dejectedly. "I'm really discouraged."

But Bob, glowing from more than just the heat as he told the story, said to the volunteer, "That's great! Look, before you came into his life a few weeks ago, that kid didn't care enough about school even to bother to cheat. Now he does. Don't you see what progress he is making? All we have to do now is channel this newly found desire to achieve and please into a willingness to work to accomplish the goal rather than cheat to attain it."

The volunteer took new heart and continued the arduous process of changing a life. Like most of Bob's volunteers, he succeeded in an area where we have previously known little but failure and repeat crimes.

Bob, like Dick Simmons a strongly Christ-centered man, has matched hundreds of volunteers on a one-to-one basis in his Partners program. He is Bill's friend and my friend. We share another treasure.

There is Fred Ress, the slim leader from the north, his long hair ending somewhere and his beard beginning somewhere else — but where? As a college student and conscientious objector Fred had applied for alternative service rather than enter the armed forces. He was assigned to the Wilderness Canoe Base in northern Minnesota run by the Plymouth Youth Center, a division of the American Lutheran Church.

I first became acquainted with Fred when I received an envelope from the Minneapolis-based Youth Center in April 1972. In it was a formal proposal for funds that would enable Fred to take a group, comprising both juvenile offenders and "positive" kids who had not been in trouble, on canoe trips into the wilderness of northern Minnesota and Canada. His proposal intrigued me because I too had been working with young offenders; ten years earlier I too had made the rugged canoe voyage from just north of Lake Superior to the James Bay area of Hudson Bay.

One of the sentences in Fred's accompanying letter went straight to my heart: "They [the troubled youth] will come back proud of what they have accomplished rather than ashamed of having been in jail or prison."

Proud of accomplishment rather than ashamed of failure — how simple and how true, I thought.

I wrote to Fred immediately that not only would I try to help obtain the necessary funds, but also I would like to accompany him on one of his shorter adventures. Four months later Fred, two court youngsters from Minneapolis, my own three sons, a probation officer and a lawyer from Topeka, Kansas, and I hoisted canoes, packs, and other gear onto our backs and headed into a lush virgin pine forest north of Lake Superior and near the Canadian border.

During our first night together around the campfire we talked about a similar trip Fred had taken the summer before. With a combination of imprisoned youngsters, "positive" kids, and kids who would probably get into trouble in the future, Fred had paddled and portaged for seventy-three days from Lake Superior to Hudson Bay.

Fred told us about "Ed," a noisy, somewhat silly sixteen-year-old who at the start of the trip was ignored by the rest of the boys. During one of their regular evening group discussions each boy remarked that Ed was the last person he would want to be on a trip with alone.

"Why?" asked Fred as he glanced at Ed leaning casually against a nearby tree.

Ed, they said, was different. He didn't want or need friends. He didn't care if people liked him, and he didn't want to like others.

After they had talked like this for some time with Ed listening, Fred asked, "Do you think that perhaps Ed wants friends too much, tries too hard for friends, needs them too desperately? Does he try so hard that he becomes obnoxious and turns people off?"

They all turned toward Ed and, as his tears glistened in the firelight, all knew that what Fred said was true. From that night on Ed became one of them.

The "positive" kids too had been deeply affected by the experience. One said, "Reform school kids! Horrors! Back home I wouldn't even talk to them, let alone associate with them. But out here we are forced to. We need each other, and we may not get through the next rapids or portage if we can't get along with each other." This particular young man also suffered a temporary mild ego-crisis when he discovered that the reform-school boys were more sensitive to the needs of others, more responsive, and more perceptive than he was.

One long-haired, fuzz-faced boy, a deeply troubled sixteen-year-old, perhaps best described the effect of Fred and their wilderness experience. "Fred taught us how to love on that trip," he said. "He taught us that when you really love someone and he loves you, you can hurt each other by what you say and do. Fred, I, and all the rest of us can really hurt each other."

Standing together at 3 a.m., our campfire sizzling and sputtering from a driving rain, Bill and I shared another treasure — a friendship with Fred Ress, a young man who is really praising the Lord and loving kids.

Walter Ungerer too became our friend, in some ways the most remarkable mutual friend Bill and I have. Walt was born in Brooklyn, New York, and reared in a cold-water flat by his hard-working parents. A very tough kid, Walt became deeply involved in street gangs at an early age and quickly battled and bullied his way to gang leadership.

As we all sweated together in our small redwood room, Walt, a burly man with a strong, demanding smallpox- and knife-scarred face, told us about the bleeding and critically wounded comrades and "enemies" he and his gang had left lying in the streets after their frequent "rumbles" with rival gangs. Though he never knew whether he had critically injured anyone or not, the thought that he may have scars his soul to this day.

Walt sat on our hot, hard wet bench and told us how, on a sultry autumn evening, he and his gang were to meet a cross-town rival. A big rumble was planned, and there was little doubt that several kids, perhaps Walt himself, would die. But the other gang did not show up, so to pass the time, Walt and his gang verbally tormented and physically abused several Presbyterian and Baptist lay people preaching on a nearby street corner.

The youths laughed and howled at and shoved and jostled the lay people as the latter told about the love of Christ. But as Walt grabbed one quiet weak-looking young man by his lapels, the man looked right into Walt's eyes and with compassion and strength in his voice said, "Christ loves you."

The words stabbed at Walt's heart. He had never before thought of anyone loving him. He let go of the man and quickly slunk off.

Walt could not sleep that night. The layman's words raced through his mind as he fitfully tossed and turned. Finally in the tranquil predawn hours, he gave his life to Christ. He miraculously escaped gang life and, after a deep struggle to learn how to read, completed college and divinity school and is now a minister.

Bill was deeply impressed with Walt, but then who wouldn't be, after hearing this man's man and God's man and his incredible story? As we listened to him, our bodies glistening with sweat, I knew that Bill, as with Jim Conley, "Ike" Simmons, Bob Moffit, Fred Ress, and others, was truly inspired by Walt.

When I think of these friends and many others doing so much for apprehended offenders, I think of what Dan Logan, founder of the "Y-Pals" volunteer program in Kansas City, Missouri, once told me. Dan said, "I am only one. *But I am one.* I will not let what I cannot do prevent me from doing what I can do — to make this a better world, if only for one other person."

Yet, as great as those moments were with our friends in the sauna, the greatest times were when we were alone — just the two of us.

On one of these occasions I told Bill about my first Christmas away from home. I will never forget it: Anchorage, Alaska, 1944.

I was alone, so very alone. During basic training and for some time thereafter I had been with a great group of guys. Abruptly I got separated from all of them and was sent to Anchorage. I arrived a few days before Christmas.

I walked about the base on Christmas Eve, my mood matching the pitch blackness of the night. As I looked up at the stars, however, they suddenly seemed to draw closer and glow brighter. I immediately felt good. I had the urge to run, and the Scripture verse came to mind, "They shall run and not be weary, they shall walk and not faint" (Isa. 40:31).

If I could have been in a race right then, I'd have beaten anyone. It was twenty-five degrees below zero, and I wore army boots and a jacket — which I soon shed because I grew hot while running. I must have run five miles that night and indeed I did not grow weary or faint.

I have never felt really alone since then, and that experience convinced me I am truly never alone. Even during the next eighteen months in the Aleutian Chain and Alaska, I did not feel alone.

In the sauna I prayed silently that Bill could feel the sustaining presence of God and could also "run and not be weary." I realized all of a sudden that I was barely nineteen years old when I had that great experience in the Frozen North — scarcely older than another youth who a generation later was to run in an hour of need.

VIII
Between My Father and His Son

ONLY A FEW MINUTES BEFORE HE DIED, MY FATHER suddenly sat up in bed and shouted to the doctor and me, "Get the gunpowder! Get the gunpowder — hurry — hurry — get the gunpowder!" It was the last thing he said to us.

Those words remain a mystery to me. Was he reliving a boyhood experience? Not likely, said his brother, Ed, when I told him about it later. They had never used gunpowder on the farm. Something he had read? He did love history and occasionally read historical novels. Was his mind simply losing touch with reality at the very end? Thus his life which really was not too complex ended in mystery.

I remember the sheer pride that I felt knowing I was his son. For a while he had to live and work in Detroit while my mother, sister, and I still lived 150 miles away in Grand Rapids, Michigan. As soon as dad drove into the driveway each Friday night, I would immediately hand him a bat and ball. He had barely enough time to say hello to my mother and sister before my friends and I trotted out into the street where he hit the baseball to us. What filled me with pride was the fact that, even though other fathers on the block returned home *every* night, he was the first father to hit the ball to us since the Sunday before, when he had to return to Detroit.

All the kids waited for my dad to come home, and when he came around the block, a cheer would go up. We were about to get the best fly balls since last Sunday. That was a real thrill for me, and I will never forget it.

Sometime ago I was in an eastern state helping a city begin to use volunteers in its court. The man who inspired the community to invite me — and who later got the program going in that city — had a sign on the desk in his office: "The most important gift a father can give to his children is to love their mother."

I do not think I fully understood the greatest gift my father gave to my sister and me until that moment.

If any husband ever loved his wife, William James "Jim" Leenhouts really loved Dorothy Champion Leenhouts. It was a beautiful love affair. They seemed always to seek common interests and pleasures, and they were patient and kind with each other. They seldom argued.

Their life together was a personification of the great love chapter of the Bible, — Corinthians 13. "Love suffers long and is kind; love envies not; love does not vaunt itself, does not behave itself unseemly, seeks not her own, is not easily provoked, thinks no evil; rejoices not in iniquity, but rejoices in the truth; bears all things, believes all things, hopes all things, endures all things. Love never fails. . . . And now abides faith, hope, love, these three; but the greatest of these is love" (cf. American Standard Version).

How my dad loved his wife! — and this love came shining through in all he said and did. He was proud of her talents in music and would sit by the hour and listen to her play the piano. He was never happier than when we had company who loved to sing. Poor dad, he couldn't carry a tune, and his favorite joke about himself was, "I don't dare sing the national anthem. With my voice, it's treason." Nevertheless, he would sit and listen to the rest of us singing while mother played the piano. He glowed with joy and satisfaction at moments like that.

He was also proud of mother when she began to teach religious education in the public schools.

Shortly after my mother's death and while I was still judge, a police officer entered my office. "I just heard about your mother," he said with tears in his eyes, "and I'm very sorry.

"I had a bad early life," he continued. "My father was an alcoholic, and he and my mother separated. My mother had to work hard to support us, and we didn't have much time with her — we were sort of left to take care of ourselves.

"I think I could well have gone on to a life of crime and, in fact, did start to get into some trouble. But when I was in third grade a wonderful lady began to come to our school and tell us stories about Jesus and the Bible. She really changed my life.

"Now I am a Christian and also I am a policeman, because I think I can serve Christ better as a cop than in any other way. But it was all because of that teacher I had in grade school, and that teacher was your mother. She gave me the greatest gift I have ever received in my life — Christ."

It was one of the great moments in my life. To hear this police officer, strong and tall in his late twenties, tell me this with tears in his eyes made me very proud of my mother.

Yet I remember thinking at that very moment of my father. How many men during that generation would have encouraged their wives to live fully and abundantly? He was always so filled with love and pride for her that there remained no room for selfishness or envy.

It was his love that brought her life to its fullest. I realize that more and more. Can there be great motherhood in its fullest sense without great fatherhood?

My father gave me a second great gift which I also did not comprehend fully until later in life. At the funeral home after dad's death in 1955, John Bosshard, a man I had worked with in Detroit during summers while going to college, told me, "You have something really great to look forward to. Up to now your dad has been alive and you have not been with him unless you were physically together. Because of our nature you really couldn't be together when you were physically separated.

"Now that is changed. The physical barriers have been removed. You can be with him all the time — spiritually. It will take a while for the new relationship to begin — maybe weeks, months, or even a few years. But it will come, and you will feel closer to him than ever before. You will be together all the time, not as it was during his lifetime when you were together only when you were physically in each other's presence.

"Actually there is good biblical authority for this," John went on. "In His lifetime Christ told the disciples that they could not understand now. They had ears, but they could not hear. They had eyes, but they could not see. But Christ promised to send a Comforter, His spiritual presence, which would be with them forever. Then they would understand.

"It is amazing. The disciples felt closer to Him, understood Him, and were helped by Him more after His death than during His life."

The second gift was presented to me about six months after my father's death. Suddenly I discovered what Johnny Bosshard meant. A new relationship was born. My father had lived his life in such a manner that he would never die in my life. Love is immortal, and his love could not die as long as I had life. Such love simply is not subject to the laws of death.

From that day until this, my father is very much alive in my life. I have a meaningful relationship with him even now, a score of years later. Could I live my life in such a way that Bill and his brothers would never really experience my death, even after they laid me away in the grave? I hope so. It is one of the great goals of fatherhood. It is attainable, but we have to work at it. It doesn't just happen.

Consider a house: The lumber and bricks do not just happen to fly together and then stick together, the right way. You have to work at it. My dad had succeeded incredibly well. Could I? I knew that working at fatherhood was the only way. It was not work of an unwanted sort. But still it was work.

A motivating force for me in working at fatherhood was the fact that Bill lost both grandfathers when he was very young. I idolized my grandfathers. When I was about five years old, had someone asked me what God was like, I would have replied unhesitatingly, "Like grandfather."

It would have been a problem for me to say which grand-father. Cornelius Leenhouts was a retired farmer, tall, gray, erect, awesome, infinitely kind and tender in the mellowness of his old age. A godlike person. When the family gathered, my place was on grandfather's lap.

Ed Champion was a saint. Everyone loved him, and he loved everyone. He lived to serve and please others. He didn't look as godlike as Cornelius, but he acted even more like that in his virtues and kindness.

I regretted that Bill would not know the influence of my dad or Audrey's dad.

My experience with my father's death, and later with my mother after her death, has caused me in recent years to ask myself, "Who really is dead? Who really is alive?" I am not sure I know.

In the building where I work there are other offices. I often say hello to the men and women who work in those offices. They are physically alive. So am I. Yet I am of little or no conse-quence in their lives. And they have little or no effect upon my life. Others they have known and loved, and others whom I have known and loved, have been declared legally dead and have been buried. Yet these deceased persons are very much alive in their lives and mine, and we are really dead in the lives of each other. Do we truly know who is alive and who is dead? I'm not sure anymore.

Another great gift dad gave me was an ability to see greatness in others and a desire to pattern my life after that greatness, real or imagined. I remember once, when I was about eleven years old, meeting the legendary Fielding H. Yost, the renowned Michigan football coach. We went over to the players' bench at the University of Michigan football stadium after the game, and my dad introduced himself. What an incredible thrill as I watched one of my heroes shake dad's hand! Then dad intro-duced me, and we shook hands. I had always seen Fielding Yost through my father's eyes, and no matter how great he really was, he was not so great as I thought he was. I aspired to the greatness that I felt in the life of "Hurry-Up" Yost.

When you live with others, you can see and understand their weaknesses as well as their strengths. Like everyone else, my father had weaknesses. Yet, he did not have a need to build himself higher in my esteem by dragging others down. He let my heroes be heroes: Lou Gehrig, Will Rogers, Charley Gehringer, Joe Louis, Dutch Clark. They were human beings with frailties, yet my dad never derogated them in any way so that he could appear to be greater. He didn't have to. When you are really great, you don't have to knock others down to improve your relative position.

Seeing greatness in others is, of course, an advantage and a disadvantage all at the same time. In seeking to persuade judges, probation officers, and wardens to use volunteers, I have to believe in people.

This realization broke upon me on a trip to California. A man who had worked with volunteers in our court in the early 1960s, and who had helped us research the effectiveness of volunteers, moved to the West Coast. In early 1967, when distrust of the volunteer concept was still prevalent, we went together to meet with a group of professionals in courts and corrections. Few volunteers were being used anywhere in the country, and California seemed the most suspicious and hostile state of all. The coldest and least responsive audience I ever faced was in Los Angeles in 1966. Hostility filled the air that night — and twelve months later, as I joined my friend, I discovered the attitude and atmosphere had changed little.

After the meeting, however, a judge came to us and said he would give the concept a try. As we left, my companion confided to me, "I wonder what he wants. He probably is going to use volunteers because he wants to build his reputation so he can get a promotion to a higher court. He might even want to become attorney general, or governor, or something like that."

I was appalled. I had had only one reaction: "Thank you, God. Here is a man who wants to help the offenders who appear before his court."

I said to my friend, "Isn't it strange? I would never have thought of that. I am just glad he is going to help those whom he has been only punishing in the past."

My associate then went on to say, "It's my mother! She has made me so suspicious of everyone. Because of her I can't think anything good about anyone. I immediately question the motivation of people."

I may not do this enough. I usually trust people and take their words to mean what they say. True, sometimes I'm disappointed in them. But continually to question the motivation of everyone — what a way to live! My dad did not instill this in me. I am so glad he did not make me into that kind of person.

When I related this incident to another friend of mine, a man in his eighties who has learned much from life, he said, "You can tell more about the motivation of people by the motivation they impute to others than in any other way." When I thought about my experiences in California, this made much sense. My associate that day would not, I am sure, do anything just to help someone else. There would have to be something in it for him. Thus, this being his sole motivation in life, how could he believe that anyone else would have any other motivation? He could not. It was that simple.

This innate trust in people has involved me in some trouble on occasion, but I am grateful that my father brought me up in such a way that I can sense greatness in others and not tear them down by questioning their motivation when this greatness finds expression in their giving of themselves to others.

Could my fatherhood be as meaningful and effective to our son Bill as dad's fatherhood had been with me? I don't know. It was a tough act to follow, as they say in show business. I thought about the verse in the Bible which says, "Every one to whom much is given, of him will much be required" (Luke 12:48). I had been given a truly great father. Could I be a truly great, or even just a good, father myself?

Years ago I heard a speaker say this: "My father taught me never to love or trust anyone. 'Don't ever let anyone become a close friend,'" he said. "He told me that if anyone became a really close friend and I trusted and loved him, he might be able to gyp me out of my money. I might lose my hard-earned money because of him. So I followed his advice. I never trusted anyone, I never loved anyone, I never really had a friend. Now I am an old man. I am lonely and empty. My life has never been anything but drudgery. But I never had anyone cheat me out of a dime and I have a lot of money now. And that's important, my dad always said.

"Somehow, now, I wish I had less money and at least one friend to love me. I am so alone. I really have nothing."

My dad, I repeat, had weaknesses. One was a deep distrust of doctors. I did not know why until later in my life when I found out that as a boy he had stepped on a rusty nail on the farm. Infection set in and spread. Finally the doctors decided that they would have to cut off his leg. The decision to amputate was final; there was nothing else they could do, they said. The operation, to be performed in the kitchen of the farmhouse, was scheduled for the next afternoon, and I can imagine my dad's fear as he waited.

Fortunately a great-aunt who lived nearby heard of the trouble and the decision. She rushed over with herbs and roots and made a poultice for my father's leg. By the time the doctor arrived the next day to perform the surgery, the swelling was down and the color was returning to normal. The surgery was delayed and, as my dad recovered, ultimately cancelled.

My dad never went to a doctor after that. We urged him to have a physical examination, but he adamantly refused. Finally, during his last illness he relented, but by then his kidneys and other organs were weak from many years of high blood pressure. There was little a doctor could do then.

Like the rest of us, dad was the product of his experiences. His thinking processes, his emotions, his abilities were shaped and limited by the circumstances of living. The reality of this was vividly demonstrated one day when I came home from high school disgusted with one of my teachers.

"I think I'll hit that teacher right in the face," I told dad. My father was not prone to overreaction, but this time he delivered a long, impassioned lecture on respecting authority. The more he talked, the angrier he became until my mother had to calm him down.

Years later I learned my dad had never finished high school in the traditional sense. He had fought — whether physically or verbally I do not know — with a teacher in high school and was expelled. He did not return, although he did get a certificate of high-school education after his discharge from the army.

I didn't know at the time I complained why my words put such fear into his heart. Of course, I was merely venting my disgust, but I soon discovered that when I wanted to relieve myself of anger and hostility toward a teacher, I had better do it to my mother when dad was not around.

Dad had an awe of education that many persons, lacking it, have. This awe led to anxiety when I did poorly in school, no matter what grade I was in. It created some hard feelings between us, because he was so anxious for me to succeed and I did not comprehend his nervousness and irritation for what it was — frustrated love and hope for my future.

The more he helped me, particularly in arithmetic, the worse I got. Fortunately my mother made me understand more and more that his worry was really love; she made dad understand that all of life is not education and all of education is not arithmetic.

Then came the great day. I awoke that morning and heard my dad on the telephone.

"Yes, that's right!" he was shouting into the phone. "He passed the bar examination."

I heard the phone click, and then heard the dialing sound again, then again, each time followed by the same excited words. I went downstairs.

"Dad, you shouldn't be bothering people at this time of the morning. It's only seven o'clock. You're waking people up."

But there was no stopping the proud father. His son was now a lawyer. I guess I never really understood that morning until Bill and his brothers explained it to me with their defeats and victories.

My dad was a banker and trust official. He spent much of his time defending the defenseless. Veterans of World War I who had been emotionally and mentally damaged in battle needed someone to look after their interests. Dad administered the trust funds for many veterans, and I became proud of this at an early age. To defend the defenseless, to help the helpless, to father the fatherless became the greatest thing you could possibly do. To be like my dad, someday in some way, became the great goal.

My dad taught me another valuable lesson. Joy is found, not in the pursuit of pleasure, but in the fulfillment of duties. This sounds rather grim, but it was true in his life and is true in mine.

Golf provides an illustration. Dad took up golf before I was born. As I grew up, he quit the game. His recreation turned to throwing the football to me, hitting fly balls to my friends and me, taking me to athletic events, and being with my sister and me. The golf bag collected more and more dust each year, and he never played the game again.

I too played golf before Bill (who is named after my father) was born and when he was young. And when Bill turned three, I put my clubs away. I didn't do it grudgingly or with a feeling of sacrifice; golf simply wasn't appropriate or fun any more. It was never "my game." I didn't touch my clubs again until Bill's brother, Dave, started to play some fifteen years later.

It is amazing, when you think about it, that deep and true happiness for me has never come through the pursuit of pleasures. Happiness has always been in the fulfillment of duties to others. Pleasure is diversion. True joy and happiness lie in fulfilling duties and obligations.

My dad also showed an intense interest in others. Whenever we went on a trip we would stay at a tourist home. Often the rest of the family would go to a movie, but not Dad. He would sit on the porch and talk for long periods about the things that most interested the owner of the tourist home. He listened with sincere attention and made other persons feel important. He *was* interested. He heightened the dignity of others by listening with genuine desire and ability to hear and to understand.

And dad gave to me the greatest gift of all. When I read and heard that God is like a father, I wanted to be with God. If God was like a father, He was powerful, loving, good, kind, and great. He had to be, because He is like a father and that is exactly what my father was.

Could I give these great gifts of love to Bill and his brothers? Fatherhood? It doesn't just happen. You have to work at it. Like nearly everything else in life, that which is the greatest achievement requires the greatest effort. Could I succeed?

IX

The Awesome Power of Love

I RAN, STAGGERED, AND WALKED WITH MY FRATER-
nity of running spectators to the two-mile mark, where we
waited anxiously for the first runner to burst from the trees.
I knew that as Bill's spikes trampled the soft pine needles on the
forest floor, his heart was in the right place and he was exerting
an incredible amount of labor where his heart was. But would
he need a greater source of strength than his own skills and
desire? Could he draw that strength from my great feeling of
love for him?

I know so many who have drawn on the awesome power of
love — love of God, love of fellowman, love of parents for
children, love of a man for his wife. Indeed, I had drawn on
that awesome power myself. What an incredible source of
energy and unbelievable strength — a power of the heart that
can transcend physical barriers!

Bill could understand this, for we had lived a life of love and
had already drawn on its power to sustain him through his early
academic and athletic defeats. I had also shared with Bill some
of the inspirational, awesome moments of love that I myself
had witnessed or experienced, such as the lesson I learned on
the day my mother died.

I HAD SPENT MANY NIGHTS AT THE HOSPITAL DURing the last three weeks of mother's life. The cancer had already ravaged the inside of her body; she was slipping fast, so the early morning call came as no surprise. "You'd better come right away, Judge Leenhouts," the nurse said. "I'm afraid your mother's condition is growing rapidly worse."

When I rushed into the sterile, sickly green hospital room moments later, mother's thin white lips quivered into a weak smile and, through tremendous effort and love, she opened her beautiful brown eyes very wide. Several times during the day I suggested that she close her eyes and try to rest. But she would feebly shake her head, strain to open her eyes even wider, and murmur words I could not understand.

At two o'clock in the afternoon my wife, the special nurse we had enlisted, and I decided I should leave to meet my sister flying in from Boston. When my sister and I returned from the airport two hours later, my wife intercepted us in the hall to tell us that, even as my footsteps still echoed in the hospital corridor as I left, mother closed her eyes and slipped into a deep coma. She had absolutely refused to go into that coma as long as her son was in the room. What incredible power and strength in her love!

My sister and I entered the still room where the irregular, labored movement of our mother's chest and the rasping respiration were all that remained of her living. At five o'clock the nurse urged my sister and me to leave the room and get a sandwich. But I just raised my head from my folded hands and shook it.

Half an hour later the nurse again urged us to go. But we did not want to leave mother. Finally at six both my wife and the nurse urged us to go, and we reluctantly agreed.

They told us later they could still hear our voices in the hall at the moment mother died.

Mother had absolutely refused to die until her daughter and son had left the room. I was overwhelmed then and still am. Mother's love had literally reached back from the grave itself to bestow a final blessing on those she loved the most — sparing her children the sight of her death. This, her final gift, had come from the same source whence all her gifts had come — the awesome power of her undying love.

I shared with Bill another story I had heard long ago — a story of a father-son love — and we discussed it many times in our sauna bath of sweat.

A young man played, or I should say practiced, football at an Ivy League university. "Jerry" wasn't skilled enough to play more than occasionally in the regular-season games, but in four years this dedicated, loyal young man never missed a practice.

The coach, deeply impressed with Jerry's loyalty and dedication to the team, also marveled at his evident devotion to his father. Several times the coach had seen Jerry and his visiting father laughing and talking as they walked arm in arm around the campus. But the coach had never met the father or talked with Jerry about him.

During Jerry's senior year and a few nights before the most important game of the season — a traditional rivalry that matched Army-Navy, Georgia-Georgia Tech, or Michigan-Ohio State in intensity — the coach heard a knock on his door. Opening it, he saw the young man, his face full of sadness.

"Coach, my father just died," Jerry murmured. "Is it all right if I miss practice for a few days and go home?"

The coach said he was very sorry to hear the news and, of course, it was all right for him to go home. As Jerry murmured a "thank you" and turned to leave, the coach added, "Please don't feel you have to return in time for next Saturday's game. You certainly are excused from that too." The youth nodded and left.

But on Friday night, just hours before the big game, Jerry again stood in the coach's doorway. "Coach, I'm back," he said, "and I have a request. May I please start the game tomorrow?"

The coach tried to dissuade the youth from his plea in the light of the importance of the game to the team. But he finally consented.

That night the coach tossed and turned. Why had he said yes to the youth? The opposing team was favored to win by three touchdowns. He needed his best players in for the entire game. Suppose the opening kickoff came to Jerry and he fumbled. Suppose he started the game and they lost by five or six touchdowns.

Obviously he could not let the youth play. It was out of the question. But he had promised.

So as the bands played and the crowd roared. Jerry stood at the goal line awaiting the opening kickoff. *The ball probably won't go to him anyway*, the coach thought to himself. Then the coach would run one series of plays, making sure the other halfback and the fullback carried the ball, and take the youth out of the game. That way he wouldn't have to worry about a crucial fumble, and he would have kept his promise.

Oh no! the coach groaned as the opening kickoff floated end over end right into Jerry's arms. But instead of fumbling, as the coach expected, Jerry hugged the ball tightly, dodged three onrushing defenders, and raced to midfield before he was finally tackled.

The coach had never seen Jerry run with such agility and power, and perhaps sensing something, he had the quarterback call Jerry's signal again. The quarterback handed off, and Jerry responded by breaking tackles for a twenty-yard gain. A few plays later he carried the ball over the goal line.

The favored opponents were stunned. Who was this kid? He wasn't even in their scouting reports, for he had up to then played a total of three minutes all year.

The coach left Jerry in, and he played the entire first half on both offense and defense. Tackling, intercepting and knocking down passes, blocking, running — he did it all.

At half time the underdogs led by two touchdowns. As for the amazed coach — in words Carl Sandburg wrote of Lincoln, "Often with nothing to say, he said *nothing*." What wisdom in these simple words!

During the second half Jerry continued to inspire the team. When the final gun sounded, his team had won.

In the locker-room bedlam reserved only for teams that have fought the impossible fight and triumphed, the coach sought out Jerry and found him sitting quietly, head in hands, in a far corner.

"Son, what happened out there?" the coach asked as he put his arm around him. "You can't play as well as you did. You're just not that fast, not that strong, or that skilled. What happened?"

Jerry looked up at the coach and said softly, "You see, coach, my father was blind. This is the first game he ever saw me play."

I like to tell this story in the sauna, because you can't tell the tears from the sweat.

The power of love. One of our very early volunteers in Royal Oak, a psychiatrist, demonstrated what that awesome power can do for offenders. I have told Bill what this psychiatrist did for "Pete," a seventeen-year-old brought before the court.

Pete was a pervert. He became involved, in effect, in a lover's quarrel with another male, and this led to his arrest for fighting. The court had no money for helping Pete with his problems, but my psychiatrist friend, like so many others in the Royal Oak area, volunteered his time to help Pete.

The doctor hospitalized Pete and treated him daily for six weeks. At the end of that time Pete left the hospital and came to see me. "I'm cured," he announced proudly.

"Great, Pete!" I replied. But I really couldn't believe it, so I called the psychiatrist and asked him if it were true.

"Yes," he said, "it's true. Pete is cured of his main problem. He has other problems, of course, but give him to one of your finest volunteers for a year or so. Let him help Pete with the problems we all have — loneliness, boy-girl relations, employment — then you can dismiss his case, for he will be all right."

"How on earth did you ever bring about this miracle?" I asked, incredulous.

The psychiatrist laughed and gently chided me. "Don't you read your Bible, Keith? I don't go to church, but you do. You should know the answer to that question. I shouldn't have to tell you.

"The story in the Bible tells how some men carried a sick and paralyzed friend over dirty, bumpy paths to the house where

Christ was preaching and healing," he continued. "Unable to get in the door because of the crowd, they carried the man to the rooftop and through an opening lowered him on a stretcher to the feet of Christ.

"Looking at him with compassion, pity, but most of all, with love, Christ said, 'Your sins are forgiven.' The man got up and walked away.

"What happened? He had overcome the guilt complex that had literally paralyzed him. The same thing happened with Pete. His parents neither wanted him nor loved him. He felt that he was bad, that he would always be bad. Indeed, his parents had told him this all his life. And he believed that all his teachers, friends, and everyone else felt the same way. He was paralyzed, emotionally, just as much as the man on the stretcher was physically paralyzed two thousand years ago. And like that man, when the guilt complex was removed, Pete was made whole once again.

"All I did was love him and try to help him overcome his guilt complex so that he could love himself. The only thing I don't understand is how Christ could do this instantaneously. It took me six intense weeks, and that was the fastest I've ever heard of it being done."

Unfortunately this miracle-working psychiatrist himself lived a sad and short life. He died, still a relatively young man, eleven years after helping Pete. The last time I saw him, the psychiatrist was lying in a hospital bed — his body abused by alcohol and his mind tortured by a life of bitter and profane rejection of his strict Catholic upbringing.

I told the psychiatrist he would certainly regain his strength soon. But lying there as pale as the sheets, he said, "No, Keith, I have no strength left, no power to fight this illness. I have given it all away to others. I have nothing left. Nothing! Nothing!"

As I lamented, *Physician, heal thyself*, I thought about Christ — in a crowd, jostled on every side by those who sought to be healed by His miraculous touch — suddenly stopping and saying, "Who touched Me?"

I could imagine Jesus' disciples — particularly Peter, the giant strong man who appointed himself Christ's bodyguard in such times and places — saying to themselves, *What does He mean,* "*Who touched me?*" *Hundreds of people surrounding Him, reaching for Him, fighting to get to Him, and He asks,* "*Who touched me?*" *If it weren't for us disciples, He might be crushed to death.* "*Who touched me?*" *Is He crazy?*

But then a woman in the crowd said, "Master, it is I. I knew if I but touched you, I would be healed. And now I am healed."

What mystery there has always been for me in this story! What power did Christ suddenly lose? How did He know that someone had used some of His strength?

Was Bill, running somewhere back in those woods, in a similar way drawing on the strength of my love for him? I felt exhausted. I had little strength left. Could it be?

I remembered the time I addressed our second national conference for volunteers in court and corrections programs. I wanted to tell the story of my mother's death, but I was afraid I would break down, so I was uncertain whether I should include it in my talk. As I took a walk early that morning (my address was to come about 9 a.m.), the first person I met was Bill Burnett — the first judge, as far as I knew, to use volunteers in a large city — Denver.

I told Bill my dilemma. He said, "I'll sit in the first row. If you falter, I'll finish the story for you. But you won't. You can use my strength too. I give it to you."

Several times during my speech I began to choke up. But each time I looked at Bill and recovered. I really drew on his power.

When it was all over, Bill said, "I'm completely exhausted. I can't even get up." He was still sitting, and I had never seen him so pale, drawn, and tired.

Or was Bill perhaps drawing on the strength and love of an even higher power, a Power that had sustained me several times in my life — as in Houston, Texas, in 1966?

Only two courts that I knew of had made a substantial and continuing use of volunteers by 1966 — Royal Oak, Michigan, and Boulder, Colorado. A few others had tried the idea on a small basis, but it didn't seem to last. Nearly everyone else thought it an absurd idea. "Volunteers? They won't stick to it," they would say. "They don't know as much as the professionals." As with everything else that is new, optimistic, and progressive, we heard the voice of thousands of "can'ts."

Houston was filled with "can'ts" too, but there were a very few "cans." Fortunately one of the "cans" was U.S. District Court Judge Woodrow Seals, a renowned and distinguished American. He and a few of his friends invited me to speak before a large Methodist congregation about this new idea of volunteers in courts.

The trip to Houston was physically, mentally, and emotionally grueling. I first spent a long afternoon speaking in Lubbock. Then it was on to Houston. After that, I had to speak in Beaumont, Bryan, and Tyler, mostly to roomfuls of "can'ts." My itinerary called for eight talks and meetings in four days. Because of my responsibilities as a judge, I left as late as possible on Friday and returned as early as I could Tuesday evening.

I arrived in Houston on a Saturday night. A group of five ministers and their wives met me, and while eating dinner at a very nice restaurant, they offered to drive me around Houston. I readily agreed, for I like to see the history of an area through the eyes of a native.

But as we got into the car, one of the ministers said, "By the way, Judge, the first sermon tomorrow — the one which you will deliver — will be televised and you must speak for exactly twenty-two minutes. The second service won't be televised, so exact time won't be a problem."

I was shocked. I hadn't known I was to appear on television and, furthermore, I had never precisely timed my speech about what volunteers in courts can do and had done in our city. I told my host I had better return to my motel, because I had a lot of work to do.

Alone in my room, I timed my speech. More than twenty-five minutes! The content was all right, but I had to cut three minutes. I tried for a second time, but both the altered content and time were miserably off the mark. And they were the third time also.

I dropped to my knees and prayed, "Lord, if you want me to talk for twenty-two minutes tomorrow, you'll have to help me do it. I'm so tired. I just have to go to bed, because if I don't get a good night's sleep, I won't be able to speak at all. So it's up to you, Lord."

The alarm awoke me from restful sleep the next morning, and I felt calm and peaceful as I rode to the church. Thirty minutes later I entered the huge, crowded church made hot by the bright television lights beaming from the balcony. After the hymns, announcements, and prayers, I stood to talk and, as I strode to the pulpit, knew that "the whole world's in His hands."

Suddenly I felt as if I were in a trance. I became totally unnecessary, for the words that I spoke could have come from the mechanics of throat, voice, and breath of any person in that room. The voice I heard — and recognized vaguely as being my own — spoke for exactly twenty-two minutes. The second I stopped, the television lights went out. The strength of God's love alone had carried me through those twenty-two minutes.

That same power of love and faith helped me in a similar situation some two years later. I was working at my desk in 1968 when the phone rang and an unfamiliar voice said, "Hello, Judge. My name is Rhett Maxwell, and I'm calling from Bethlehem, Pennsylvania. If you possibly could, we'd really like to have you come to Bethlehem on the second Friday night and Saturday morning in December to help us start a volunteer program in our court."

I had never heard of Mr. Maxwell and explained to him that I tried hard not to be away from home on weekends. I was perfectly willing to work sixty hours a week from Monday morning to Friday late afternoon, but my weekends were devoted to family, Sunday school, and church. I tried to adhere strictly to this self-imposed rule and violated it only about five times a year.

"But, Judge," Mr. Maxwell continued, "please let me explain what is behind this call. Several months ago I read the story about Royal Oak's volunteer program in *Reader's Digest** and decided we needed a program like that in Bethlehem. I went to the court and tried to persuade the judge to begin a volunteer program. But he simply said, 'Mr. Maxwell, it's a crazy idea. I don't care what the *Digest* says, I'm sure volunteers don't work in Royal Oak and I'm sure they won't work here. So please do us both a favor and forget it.'"

But Rhett Maxwell, an executive of Bethlehem Steel Corporation, is a Christ-centered man who does not just forget about ideas that are right and good. He went home and thought and prayed. A few days later he returned to the court and sought out the judge.

"Judge," he began, "I understand you're a bit of a gambler. Well, so am I. I occasionally play golf for fifty cents a hole with my friends, just as you do. Every bid I make in business is a gamble. How, how about you and I betting on this volunteer program? Give me the worst, most hopeless young offender you have. Let me work with him for six months. If he doesn't improve in those six months, I'll get off your back and not bother you again. If he does improve, you lose the bet and we start a volunteer program."

The judge laughed and said, "Okay. You have a bet. You can work with 'Luis,' a seventeen-year-old Puerto Rican boy. And believe me, Mr. Maxwell, Luis is a felony looking for a place to happen and there's *no way* that you, I, or anyone else can help him."

Three months passed and Rhett grew depressed. Despite the intense love and concern he had shown daily to Luis, it looked as if Rhett would lose the bet — Luis just wasn't responding. The words *no way* rang in Rhett's ears. *Maybe I should just stick to steel and forget the whole idea,* he thought.

Rhett was learning the lesson every volunteer must learn. Who he is — often a reasonably successful person — may speak so loudly that probationers — more often the unsuccessful in

*"Royal Oak Aids Its Problem Youth," October 1965, and "Big Help for Small Offenders," April 1968.

society — can't hear what the volunteer says until he has done two things for months: first, be there; second, listen.

An upcoming family vacation complicated matters. What should he do? Should he tell the court he lost the bet and forget about Luis while on vacation? Should he call and write Luis while gone? Or should he take Luis with him on vacation?

He and his family decided on the latter. For the first time in his life Luis water-skied, swam in a lake, and more importantly, was surrounded by real family love.

The experience deeply affected and changed Luis. Toward the end of the six months he got a steady job and married his high-school sweetheart. Rhett and his wife and family were the only non-Puerto Ricans at the wedding.

Rhett returned to the court shortly after the wedding and asked, "Well, Judge, did I win or lose?"

"I just can't believe it!" the judge replied in amazement. "I have never lost a surer bet in my whole life. The odds were overwhelmingly in my favor. But I've never welshed on a bet before and I won't now. You can start your volunteer program, and I'll cooperate."

Relating this story to me over the phone, Rhett concluded, "Judge Leenhouts, I have been talking to the Lord and He says that you have to come here."

On the second Friday in December I left for Bethlehem to meet with the city officials. After I talked with them for three hours that night about the tremendous amount of work and love it takes to begin a volunteer program, Rhett got their verbal commitment.

The next morning I attended the annual meeting of Rhett Maxwell's Presbyterian Men's Club and their guests, the 150 citizens from whom would come the first group of volunteers in the new program. Rhett had personally telephoned every person in that room, urged each to attend, and stated his conviction that great things were about to happen.

Except for the absence of a time limit, the situation reminded me of Houston. The atmosphere again was charged with excitement, like the stadium for the Michigan-Ohio State game. Again I felt as though I were in a trance. Anyone else in the room would have served as a speaker just as well as I; I was simply a channel for someone else's speech — I added nothing, took nothing away.

A standing ovation erupted as I finished talking. But I could not say another word — not even "thank you." I stood there, still in a trance, nodding dumbly. As I looked at the audience standing and clapping, I could only think, *Lord, they are applauding You. I hope You are enjoying it.*

Then I noticed that many — indeed, most — of the people were crying. So was I. But I wasn't ashamed of my tears, for I remembered what Carl Sandburg once wrote of Lincoln — "he was seen to weep in a way that made weeping appropriate, decent, majestic." The city official who was supposed to acknowledge my address tried to do so, but he too was weeping. The words would not leave his mouth.

Bethlehem started its program. Rhett and the others put their hearts into a tremendous amount of hard, intelligent work.

The strength and power of God's love had sustained me in Bethlehem and Houston. I wondered what sustained Bill in his time of need — his love for God? his love for me? Could he draw strength from my great feeling of love for him?

My mind reflected on the things we had never talked about. Wealth, prestige, fame — it seems as if when you are sitting in a sauna, sweat dripping from the open pores, your skin glistening, the stomach starting to feel just a little woozy, you just don't talk about superficial things.

Somehow, perhaps it would not be appropriate to talk about those things when you are in kinship with the hearty Finnish folk who gave us this great sauna tradition. When you think of Finns you think of courage, honesty, and basic virtues; At least I always did, even before I met my wife in the American mecca of Finns, northern Minnesota.

There, where the United States and Canada meet in the simple, beautiful canoe country, men are still honored for their ability to paddle a canoe, to portage a heavy pack on rough trails between the lakes, to catch and filet fish, to scare off the bear that come into camp, and to sit by the campfire, sometimes in rain, and talk about the world's most important subject . . . nothing.

You feel a sort of rugged kinship with men — their women and children too — who endure wet feet, mosquitoes, black flies, rain, wet tents, high winds, long portages, and all the terrible things which make canoe trips in the boundary waters so glorious and great.

There was a high-school boy in my Sunday school class at one time who was a good athlete. He loved hockey, but decided to play basketball for the school team rather than enter the city hockey league. I asked him why.

"I really like hockey better," he said, "but there is more status in playing basketball for the varsity school team." I was amazed and disappointed — a high-school kid doing something he really did not want to do because there was status in it. I thought of his mother and father, and I understood. I wonder how often they talked about social standing and what others thought.

Should I have talked with Bill about these things? Would this have motivated him more than our talks about love, victory through defeat, and intense desire?

SUDDENLY THE FIRST RUNNER FLASHED BETWEEN two tall pines that framed a final gateway out of the wooded maze. I could tell again by the runner's unique stride that it was not Bill. Seconds later a second runner — *not Bill either . . . too bent over . . . Bill runs straight up . . . probably too straight up.* Another emerged from the trees, number three, and still no Bill.

In an instant I saw him, running in a virtual tie with a youth who had beaten him badly all year. My heart pounded — fourth or fifth place — either was All-State, Bill's dream! Pain, anxiety, intense desire contorted Bill's face. I had never seen him look so strained, exhausted, and physically and emotionally spent. To my worrying eyes, the other runner, younger and a grade behind Bill in school, appeared to run so much more smoothly, more relaxedly, more confidently.

I looked over at Bill's brother, Dave, who had joined me. No brother ever had a more loyal supporter than Bill and Jim did in Dave. Jim's game was hockey. Before Jim's best game the season before, Dave had diagramed the whole strategy and spent more than an hour going over it with him. And it helped, as much as the counsel of any coach. Now Dave's eyes met mine. We didn't have to say anything — both of us knew what we felt for Bill.

"Go Blue! Come on, Ba-ee!" Could he hear? Could he feel my love reaching out? Was the power of love in his heart and mind perhaps so great that, even running mechanically, it subconsciously undergirded every movement, every pain-racked breath? I wondered and worried as he disappeared from view.

As I rushed along to the 2½-mile mark, I passed close to the start-finish line where my beautiful wife stood wondering and praying. Audrey had enthusiastically supported everything Bill ever did, pouring out love and encouragement through the turmoil of Bill's grade-school years, cheering at all our Flag Football games, and attending nearly all Bill's track and cross-country meets.

Audrey and Bill early established a wonderfully close relationship. When Bill was young, I heard her mother-talk: "Put on your boots." "Be sure to comb your hair." "Thank Mrs. Logan for the nice time." I think Bill understood that all of those words really mean "I love you."

Bill and his brothers even developed a kind way of telling her they didn't like something she had cooked for them. They would eat a little bit and say, "Mom, this sure is good . . . but very filling."

Now as I ran past Audrey, she looked at me with hope and anxiety in her beautiful, misty eyes.

"He's fourth!" I choked and turned away as I felt tears welling in my own eyes. And I felt tired — so tired — propelling my legs only on nerves.

The leader — a smooth, confident runner from Grosse Pointe, a fashionable suburb of Detroit — moved effortlessly past the 2½-mile marker. The second and third men, also appearing to run easily without strain or pain, burst over the crest of the hill. All were ranked much higher than Bill on the basis of past performances, as were most of the runners there that day.

My eyes strained toward the hill as I waited for Bill and the other youth who had battled each other so closely at the two-mile mark. The other runner appeared. But where was Bill? The endless hours of running in summer and winter, the map on the basement wall — were they in vain? Would this be a final agonizing defeat?

Then over the hill Bill came, running hard and straining every muscle. Tears rushed to cool my burning eyes as I saw Bill's sweat-and-spit-covered face. (A runner needs to spit, but Bill said later that he didn't have time to turn his head.) Fifth place and All-State lay 880 yards ahead.

I focused my attention for the first time on the runners behind Bill. Good! Only two were close. He should be able to hold on and finish well within the top fifteen.

Gasping for breath, I ran toward the finish chute, two 100-foot ropes that narrowed to a V at the finish line. Everyone stood on the left of the chute, so I ducked under the ropes and dashed to an official's automobile parked on the other side.

I had just straightened up when the Grosse Pointe runner crossed the finish line to the cheers and applause of the spectators. What a great job he had done, running the grueling three-mile course in just under sixteen minutes!

Pressing against the ropes, I kept my eyes on the course as the winner received his Number One card from the officials. The second and third runners, who had led Bill for most of the race, streaked through the chute. Their positions had not changed. An eternity later Bill and his now very familiar competitor entered the chute numbly battling for fourth place over those last few yards. Both had given everything they had and a little bit more, but were still matching each other stride for stumbling stride.

Both runners crossed the finish line together. Overzealous officials, disputing who had finished fourth, grabbed their arms and roughly jerked the runners back and forth, trying to place them in official order. My face flushed hot with anger. It didn't matter if Bill was fourth or fifth — the race was over and he had made All-State. Firmness was necessary, but the over-

Bill Williams Studio-Royal Oak

Bill Leenhouts - Cross Country 1972
All-League, Metro, County and State
Coach - Richard Zulch

A picture of Bill like this one hangs in the Kimball High School Hall of Fame, reserved for All-State athletes.

reacting officials were throwing them around like police officers breaking up a fight.

I looked at Bill's face. Agony twisted his boyish features as he staggered aimlessly down the chute. Thinking he was about to collapse, I instinctively ducked under the ropes, ran to him, grabbed his arm, and put it over my shoulder.

Amid my ecstasy I felt a moment of alarm. Bill's reddened face was wet with sweat and spit; he rasped and gasped for breath uncontrollably as he staggered lifelessly against me. I had never seen him so exhausted, so completely spent. His arm hung lifeless around my shoulder, and for a few seconds we walked down the finishing chute, Bill leaning on me as helpless as he was the day we brought him home from the hospital eighteen years before.

Abruptly he straightened up and sighed, deeply. "I'm okay now, Dad." He had recovered and was ready to jog a mile or so to "warm down."

But I was overwhelmed. I tried to hold back the tears that welled in my eyes, but couldn't. And when I realized that I couldn't possibly hold them back, I just let the tears come. I wept. I tried to look at Bill, but I could not see him. I tried to talk, but the choked weeping stilled my voice.

We must have been a strange sight — the runner, completely exhausted, clinging heavily to a middle-aged man shuffling down the chute and crying as hard as a baby.

I thought I would be prepared for this moment. But how could I have prepared for the beautiful and utterly overwhelming experience of the power of love — my love for our son, his love for us — a love fulfilled in victory after a lifetime of defeats? My whole being cried out for the world to know how much I loved Bill, how proud I was of him, how defeat had finally changed to triumph, how love had conquered the odds.

I turned my back to the crowd and plodded toward the nearby woods. I walked fifty feet or more, slowly, for I could not see clearly through the tears.

At first I was ashamed to weep. My basic sense of masculinity and toughness was shattered. Yet one thought dominated: Sandburg's words of Lincoln. So, while I was ashamed, I was also proud of those tears. For me to be so overwhelmed with emotion, my facade of masculinity completely lost to the point of weeping in public, something wonderful must have occurred. Indeed, it had. Deep in my heart I knew I wept in a way that made weeping appropriate . . . decent . . . yes, one might even say, majestic.